A PRIMER

RATIONAL EMOTIVE BEHAVIOR THERAPY

Windy Dryden

Raymond DiGiuseppe

Michael Neenan

THIRD EDITION

Research Press
2612 North Mattis Avenue
Champaign, Illinois 61822
(800) 519-2707
www.researchpress.com

Composition by Jeff Helgesen
Printed by Seaway Printing Co., Inc.

ISBN-13: 978-0-87822-636-8
Library of Congress Control Number 2010925553

We dedicate this book to the memory and enduring legacy of Albert Ellis, the originator of rational emotive behavior therapy

CONTENTS

INTRODUCTION

For well over three decades, we have trained numerous mental health practitioners in the basics of rational emotive behavior therapy (REBT). During that time, we have seen the publication of many comprehensive book-length texts on REBT, including some of our own (e.g., Dryden & Neenan, 2004; Ellis & Dryden, 1997; Walen, DiGiuseppe, & Dryden, 1992). Indeed, we have used and recommended these texts in our basic REBT training programs. However, we have often found these books too lengthy for use in a basic instructional course on REBT and wished that a primer for therapists was available that could provide a concise but systematic guide to the basics of REBT practice. Such a guide was eventually published in 1990. With this third edition of the primer, we have updated certain parts of the text to reflect developments in REBT theory and practice in the last two decades.

In Part I, we briefly outline the principles we consider central to an understanding of the practical steps involved in REBT. These practical steps, outlined in Part II, are presented in the order in which we recommend you apply them in clinical work with clients and in your practice in counseling one another.* Part III illustrates the application of the REBT process to a specific case. Finally, we present two appendices. In Appendix 1, we present, in tabular form, information to help you to distinguish between unhealthy and healthy negative emotions (Dryden, 2009a), and in Appendix 2, we outline the distinctive features of REBT that help to set it apart from other psychotherapies, especially other cognitive-behavioral approaches (Dryden, 2009b).

In the complex world of clinical practice, clients rarely seek help for only one emotional problem. Rather, they more often come to treatment with several seemingly separate but interlocking problems. The brief overview of REBT practice presented in this primer is designed to complement rather than replace the comprehensive texts that can help you deal with such situations and conduct REBT at a more advanced level. We advise you to first read and digest the material in this primer, then consult the resources recommended at the end of this book for more detailed discussion of the therapeutic process. Many other useful materials on REBT can be ordered from the Albert Ellis Institute, 45 East 65th Street, New York, NY 10065–6508; telephone: (212) 535–0822; www.albertellisinstitute.org.

We hope that you will consider this primer to be a helpful introduction to REBT and that you will find REBT to be a valuable approach in helping your clients overcome their emotional and behavioral difficulties.

---

*Peer counseling is used in all the basic training programs of the Albert Ellis Institute and is an excellent way of learning to practice REBT. We strongly recommend that you consult the step-by-step guidelines in this primer regularly during peer counseling.

Part I

THEORY

In the first part of this primer, we outline some central principles of rational emotive behavior therapy (REBT), first considering the meanings of the terms *rationality* and *irrationality* as they are used in REBT. Next, we discuss REBT's well-known "Situational ABC" framework, considering each element in turn. We subsequently describe two basic biological human tendencies and two fundamental human disturbances that are relevant to the theory and practice of REBT and briefly outline the REBT theory of change.

RATIONALITY VERSUS IRRATIONALITY

In REBT, to be rational, it is necessary to be (a) flexible and nonextreme, (b) pragmatic, (c) logical, and (d) reality based. Thus rationality is defined as that which is adaptable and moderate, helps people to achieve their basic goals and purposes, is logical, and is empirically consistent with reality. Conversely, irrationality refers to that which is rigid and extreme, prevents people from achieving their basic goals and purposes, is illogical, and is empirically inconsistent with reality.

The terms *rational* and *irrational* are most often used to describe beliefs in REBT. It is important to note that these terms may have very different meanings for some clients who may particularly view the term *irrational beliefs* pejoratively. In such cases, we suggest that you use different, more acceptable terminology with such clients (e.g., helpful and unhelpful beliefs).

THE SITUATIONAL ABC FRAMEWORK

The Situational ABC framework is the cornerstone of REBT practice. Let us define and discuss each element. In doing so, we assume that your client is discussing an emotional problem.

Situation

Your client does not experience her or his emotional problem in a vacuum. Rather, she or he does so in a specific situation. In considering this situation, bear in mind that it should reflect as accurately as possible the context in which your client experienced her or his emotional problem.

A

The A in this framework stands for adversity. It refers to the aspect of the situation that your client is most disturbed about. This may be either external or internal to your client. Although A may correspond to an actual aspect of the situation that can be confirmed as accurate by neutral observers (i.e., the principle of confirmable reality), it is more often an inference about the situation or an aspect of the situation.

An inference goes beyond the data at hand and can be accurate or inaccurate. Let's assume that your client receives an e-mail from her boss that he wants to see her after lunch, and she is anxious about this. It turns out that she is most anxious about her boss criticizing her work. Her A—"My boss is going to criticize my work"—is an inference, as it goes beyond the facts of the situation. In this example, the facts are that your client's boss has indicated that he wants to see your client after lunch and that she does not know why. Her inference may be accurate or it may be inaccurate, but what makes it an inference is that it goes beyond the data at hand. Please note that when your client is anxious about her boss criticizing her work, she views this as a fact and not as an inference.

One of the major differences between REBT and other forms of cognitive-behavioral approaches is that in REBT we encourage clients to assume temporarily that their inferences at A are correct, even when they appear distorted. By contrast, in other CBT approaches, therapists may encourage clients to examine their inferences. REBT therapists take this tack because we hold that doing so encourages us to identify our clients' irrational beliefs, which, as we will presently see, we regard as lying at the core of our clients' emotional problems (see Dryden, 2009b).

B

B stands for beliefs. These are attitudes that are either rigid or flexible and extreme or nonextreme. These beliefs can be either general or specific in nature. Because this is an introductory book on REBT and we are considering the Situational ABC framework that is best used in assessing specific instances of your clients' emotional problems, we focus in this book on irrational beliefs that are specific rather than general in nature. For a discussion of general irrational beliefs, consult Walen et al. (1992).

When beliefs are rigid and extreme, they are called irrational beliefs, and when they are flexible and nonextreme, they are called rational beliefs. Let's look closely at both sets of beliefs.

Irrational Beliefs: Rigid Beliefs

More than 40 years ago, Albert Ellis (1962) argued that irrational beliefs underpin people's emotional problems in the face of life's adversities. However, perhaps his important contribution to our understanding of psychopathology is the insight that, of people's irrational beliefs, it is rigid beliefs that are at the very core of these problems (Ellis, 1994). Rigid beliefs take the form of musts, absolute shoulds, have-to's, got-to's, and so forth.

Ellis (1999, 2000) argued that although your clients will express their rigid beliefs in personally distinctive terms, you may find it helpful to consider these individualistic beliefs to be variations of three basic rigid beliefs. These involve the following types of demands:

1. Demands about self. These rigid beliefs are frequently revealed in statements such as "I must do well on my forthcoming test." Rigid beliefs about self often lead to anxiety, depression, shame, and guilt.

2. Demands about others. These rigid beliefs are often expressed in such statements as "You must treat me well when I come to see you tomorrow." Rigid beliefs about others are associated with feelings of damning anger and rage, as well as with passive-aggressiveness and acts of violence.

3. Demands about world/life conditions. These rigid beliefs are often expressed in such statements as "My homework must not be as difficult as it is." Such rigid beliefs are associated with feelings of self-pity and hurt, as well as with problems of self-discipline (e.g., procrastination or addictive behavior).

Irrational Beliefs: Extreme Beliefs

When your clients adhere to rigid beliefs, they tend to hold one or more extreme irrational beliefs that, according to REBT theory, are derived from these rigid beliefs. Let us briefly list and discuss these extreme beliefs.

"Awfulizing" beliefs

When your clients hold "awfulizing" beliefs, they believe, at the time, that the adversity at A is more than 100 percent bad, worse than it absolutely should be, and that no good can come from it. We now provide some examples of awfulizing beliefs (in italics) and show the rigid beliefs from which they are derived (in parentheses).

► ("I must do well on my forthcoming test) . . . *and it will be awful I don't.*"

► ("You must treat me well when I come to see you tomorrow) . . . *and it will be terrible if you don't.*"

► ("My homework must not be as difficult as it is) . . . *and because it is that difficult, it's the end of the world.*"

Discomfort-intolerance beliefs

When your clients hold discomfort-intolerance beliefs, they believe, at the time, that they cannot endure situations or have any happiness at all if what they demand must not exist at A actually does exist. We provide some examples of discomfort-intolerance beliefs (in italics) and show the rigid beliefs from which they are derived (in parentheses).

➤ ("I must do well on my forthcoming test) . . . *and I couldn't stand it if I don't."*

➤ ("You must treat me well when I come to see you tomorrow) . . . *and it would be unbearable if you don't."*

➤ ("My homework must not be as difficult as it is) . . . *and because it is that difficult, I can't tolerate it."*

Depreciation beliefs

When your clients hold depreciation beliefs, they tend to disparage themselves, others, and/or life conditions. We provide some examples of depreciation beliefs (in italics) and show the rigid beliefs from which they are derived (in parentheses).

➤ ("I must do well on my forthcoming test) . . . *and I am unworthy if I don't."*

➤ ("You must treat me well when I come to see you tomorrow) . . . *and you are a bad person if you don't."*

➤ ("My homework must not be as difficult as it is) . . . *and life is all bad for making it that difficult."*

Rational Beliefs: Flexible Beliefs

Albert Ellis (1962) also argued that rational beliefs underpin people's healthy responses to life's adversities and that, of these rational beliefs, it is people's flexible beliefs that are at the very core of these healthy responses (Ellis, 1994). Flexible beliefs (also called nondogmatic preferences) take the form of desires, wishes, wants, and preferences. However, what defines their flexible nature is that these beliefs are not transformed by your clients into dogmatic musts, shoulds, oughts, and so on.

Three basic flexible beliefs

In the previous section, we outlined three basic rigid beliefs. The following are the rational alternatives to such beliefs, which we call the three basic flexible beliefs.

1. Nondogmatic preferences about self. These flexible beliefs are frequently revealed in statements such as "I would like to do well on my forthcoming test, but it's not necessary for me to do so." Flexible beliefs about self often lead to concern (as opposed to anxiety), sadness (as opposed to depression), disappointment (as opposed to shame), and remorse (as opposed to guilt).

2. Nondogmatic preferences about others. These flexible beliefs are often expressed in statements such as "I would like you to treat me well when I come to see you tomorrow, but sadly and regretfully you don't have to do so." Flexible beliefs about others are associated with feelings of nondamning anger (as opposed to damning anger and rage), as well as with assertiveness (as opposed to passive-aggressiveness and acts of overt aggression).

3. Nondogmatic preferences about world/life conditions. These flexible beliefs are often expressed in statements such as "I would like my homework not to be as difficult as it is, but unfortunately it doesn't have to be the way I want it to be." Such flexible beliefs are associated with feelings of disappointment and sorrow (as opposed to self-pity and hurt), as well as with self-disciplined behavior (as opposed to problems of self-discipline such as procrastination or addictive behavior).

Please note that there are two components of flexible beliefs (or nondogmatic preferences). In the first component, your client asserts what she wants, and in the second component, she acknowledges that she does not have to get what she wants. This is the reason that flexible beliefs have the word *but* in them. Why not review the basic three flexible beliefs just presented to see what we mean?

Rational Beliefs: Nonextreme Beliefs

When your clients adhere to flexible beliefs, they tend to hold one or more nonextreme rational beliefs that, according to REBT theory, are derived from these flexible beliefs. Let us briefly list and discuss these nonextreme beliefs.

Nonawfulizing beliefs

When your clients hold nonawfulizing beliefs, they believe, at the time, (1) that things could always be worse; (2) that the adversity that they face is less than 100 percent bad; and (3) that good could come from the adversity. Following are some examples of nonawfulizing beliefs (in italics) and the flexible beliefs from which they are derived (in parentheses).

- ► ("I would like to do well on my forthcoming test, but it's not necessary for me to do so) . . . *It's bad if I don't do well, but not awful.*"

- ► ("I would like you to treat me well when I come to see you tomorrow, but sadly and regretfully you don't have to do so) . . . *It would be very unfortunate if you treat me badly, but not terrible.*"

- ► ("I would like my homework not to be as difficult as it is, but unfortunately it doesn't have to be the way I want it to be) . . . *It's a pain that it is so difficult, but not the end of the world.*"

Please note that there are two components of nonawfulizing beliefs. In the first component, your client asserts that it is bad when he does not get what he wants, and in the second component, he acknowledges that it is not terrible when this happens. Again note the word *but* in the nonawfulizing beliefs just presented.

Discomfort-tolerance beliefs

When your clients hold discomfort-tolerance beliefs, they believe, at the time, (1) that they will struggle if the discomfort continues to exist, but that they will neither die nor disintegrate; (2) that they will not lose the capacity to experience happiness if the discomfort continues to exist, although this capacity will be temporarily diminished; and (3) that the discomfort is worth tolerating. Following are some examples of discomfort-intolerance beliefs (in italics) and the flexible beliefs from which they are derived (in parentheses).

- ► ("I would like to do well on my forthcoming test, but it's not necessary for me to do so) . . . *It would be a struggle for me to stand not doing well, but I could stand it and it would be worth it to me to do so.*"

- ► ("I would like you to treat me well when I come to see you tomorrow, but sadly and regretfully you don't have to do so) . . . "*It would be difficult for me to bear your bad behavior, but I could bear it and it would be worth it to me to do so.*"

▶ ("I would like my homework not to be as difficult as it is, but unfortunately it doesn't have to be the way I want it to be) . . . *It's hard tolerating such difficulty, but I can tolerate it and it's in my best interests to do so.*"

Please note that there are three components to discomfort-tolerance beliefs. In the first component, your client asserts that it is a struggle for her to tolerate her desires not being met. In the second component, she acknowledges that she can tolerate this, and in the third component, she stresses that it is worth it to her to do so.

Please reread the discomfort-tolerance beliefs just presented so that you can identify these three components in each presented discomfort-tolerance belief.

Acceptance beliefs

When your clients hold acceptance beliefs, they will accept themselves and others as fallible human beings who cannot legitimately be given a single global rating. They will also accept the world and life conditions as being complex—composed of good, bad, and neutral elements. Thus they will also refrain from giving the world a global rating. We provide some examples of acceptance beliefs (in italics) and show the flexible beliefs from which they are derived (in parentheses).

▶ ("I would like to do well on my forthcoming test, but it's not necessary for me to do so) . . . *If I don't do well it would not mean that I am unworthy. I would be the same fallible human being whether I do well or not.*"

▶ ("I would like you to treat me well when I come to see you tomorrow, but sadly and regretfully you don't have to do so) . . . *Although I would dislike your bad behavior, it would not make you a bad person. You would be a fallible person who retains the capacity to act both badly and well.*"

▶ ("I would like my homework not to be as difficult as it is, but unfortunately it doesn't have to be the way I want it to be) . . . *It's bad that my homework is so difficult, but life is not all bad when this happens. Life is a complex mixture of the good, the bad, and the neutral.*"

Please note again that there are three components of acceptance beliefs. In the first component, your client asserts that it is bad when he does not get what he wants, or he evaluates some aspect of himself, another, or life conditions negatively. In the second component, he acknowledges that he, the other person, or life cannot be given a global rating when his desires are not met, and in the third component, he asserts the fallibility of himself and another or the complexity of life. Please reread the acceptance beliefs so that you can identify these three components in each presented acceptance belief.

C

C in the ABC framework stands for the emotional, behavioral, and cognitive consequences of your clients' beliefs about A. The C's that follow from irrational beliefs about adversities at A will be disturbed and are called unhealthy negative consequences, whereas the C's that follow from rational beliefs about adversities at A will be undisturbed and are termed healthy negative consequences (Ellis, 1994; these unhealthy and healthy negative consequences were previously called inappropriate and appropriate negative consequences, respectively).

As we said earlier, there are three consequences of beliefs: emotional consequences, behavioral consequences, and cognitive or thinking consequences. We discuss these one at a time.

C: Emotional Consequences

When an adversity occurs, your client will experience a negative emotion. REBT theory argues that if your client holds an irrational belief about the adversity at A, then he or she will experience an unhealthy negative emotion (known as a UNE in REBT). Clients seek counseling help for one or more of eight UNEs: anxiety, depression, guilt, shame, hurt, problematic anger, problematic jealousy, and problematic envy. These negative emotions tend to be unhealthy for the following reasons:

1. They lead to the experience of a great deal of psychic pain and discomfort.

2. They motivate one to engage in self-defeating behavior.

3. They prevent one from carrying out behavior necessary to reach one's goals.

4. They lead to highly distorted and other forms of dysfunctional thinking.

However, if your client held a rational belief about the same adversity, he or she would experience what we call in REBT a healthy negative emotion (known as an HNE in REBT). The healthy alternatives to the eight UNEs listed previously are as follows: concern (as opposed to anxiety), sadness (as opposed to depression), remorse (as opposed to guilt), disappointment (as opposed to shame), (sorrow as opposed to hurt), nonproblematic anger (as opposed to problematic anger), nonproblematic jealousy (as opposed to problematic jealousy), and nonproblematic envy (as opposed to problematic envy). These negative emotions tend to be healthy for the following reasons:

1. They alert one that one's goals are being blocked but do not immobilize one.
2. They motivate one to engage in self-enhancing behavior.
3. They encourage the successful execution of behavior necessary to reach one's goals.
4. They lead to balanced and other forms of functional thinking.

C: Behavioral Consequences

Behavioral consequences of holding beliefs can take the form of either overt actions or action tendencies. In an overt action, your client carries out a behavior, whereas in an action tendency, he or she experiences an urge to carry out the behavior but may not necessarily do so. When he or she does do so, we can say that he or she has converted the action tendency into an overt action.

When your client holds an irrational belief about an adversity at A, then his or her behavior at C (overt action and action tendency) will tend to be unconstructive. Human beings have the capacity to suppress their action tendencies, and when your client does this, then his or her unconstructive behavior will become clear only if you inquire about his or her action tendencies, as he or she will not have acted in any overt manner. Imagine that your client is angry and you don't know whether or not his or her anger is problematic. So you decide to assess his or her behavior, as in the following exchange:

> You: So, when you were angry in this situation, what did you do?
>
> Client: Nothing.
>
> You: What did you feel like doing, but didn't actually do?
>
> Client: I felt like smashing his face in!

As you can probably tell by the action tendency, this client's anger proved to be problematic!

When your client holds a rational belief about an adversity at A, then his or her behavior at C (overt action and action tendency) will tend to be constructive.

C: Cognitive Consequences

This primer is intended to provide a brief introduction to the theory and practice of REBT. As such, consideration of the cognitive consequences of holding beliefs is beyond our scope, as this is a more advanced topic. However, in brief, you should note that when a client holds an irrational belief about adversity, then the cognitive consequences of holding this belief (or what we call his or her "subsequent thinking") will tend to be highly distorted and skewed to the negative. On the other hand, if your client holds a rational belief about the same adversity, then subsequent thinking will tend to be balanced and will incorporate a realistic view of the situation he or she is in.

We have now outlined all the elements of the Situational ABC model. As you progress in your career as an REBT therapist, it is important for you to learn how to assess your clients' emotional problems and how to distinguish between unhealthy negative emotions (UNEs) and healthy negative emotions (HNEs). Although we cannot devote space to this important issue in this introductory primer, we do include a set of tables in Appendix 1 to which we encourage you to refer as you learn to assess your clients' problems (Dryden 2009a). In these tables, we list the most common adversities (i.e., inferences at A), irrational beliefs, behaviors, and subsequent forms of thinking associated with anxiety, depression, guilt, shame, hurt, problematic anger, problematic jealousy, and problematic envy and their healthy alternatives.

INTERACTION OF A, B, AND C

In our simple presentation of the Situational ABC framework, it is assumed that adversities (inferred or actual) at A trigger beliefs at B, which in turn lead to feelings, behaviors, and further thinking at C.

In reality, A, B, and C frequently interact in quite complex ways (Ellis, 1985). This process is known as psychological interactionism.

For example, your clients may bring rigid beliefs to a situation that lead them to create overly negative inferences at A or to focus on particular features of A that they might not attend to if they had more rational beliefs. Thus, if your clients dogmatically believe that they must not be socially rejected, they will tend to see social rejection where none really existed and focus on the negative statements others make about them to the exclusion of more neutral or positive statements. In similar fashion, having certain feelings (C's) such as depression may make it easy for clients to hold irrational beliefs at B. Furthermore, being in a certain situation may influence your clients to create irrational beliefs at B that they might not make if they were in another context. For example, being in a dark, unfamiliar room might evoke more anxiety-creating irrational beliefs than being in a well-lit, familiar room.

Because a full analysis of the ways in which A, B, and C interact is beyond the scope of this primer, we suggest that you consult the resources listed at the end of the book for further information.

TWO BASIC BIOLOGICAL TENDENCIES

Albert Ellis made the important point that people very easily tend to transform their desires into absolute musts, particularly when those desires are strong (Ellis, 1976). The fact that we seem to do this so easily and frequently led Ellis to conclude that this pattern constitutes a basic biological tendency in most, if not all, humans. Although Ellis did acknowledge that social influences also have an effect in this regard, he noted that "even if everybody had had the most rational upbringing, virtually all humans would often irrationally transform their individual and social preferences into absolute demands on (a) themselves, (b) other people, and (c) the universe around them" (Ellis, 1984a, p. 20).

As Ellis pointed out, however, humans have a second basic biological tendency: the power of choice and the ability to identify, challenge, and change irrational thinking. So, although the tendency to think irrationally may in part have a strong biological component, we are not slaves to this tendency. We can strive to overcome it by repeatedly working to change our irrational beliefs.

TWO FUNDAMENTAL HUMAN DISTURBANCES

Ellis noted that human psychological problems can be loosely divided into two major categories: ego disturbance and discomfort disturbance. Ego disturbance relates to the rigid beliefs that we hold about ourselves and the consequent self-depreciation that we engage in when we fail to live up to our self-imposed demands. Furthermore, ego-disturbance issues may underpin what at first glance appear to be rigid beliefs about others or life conditions. Thus your client may be angry with someone who is acting in a way that she perceives as a threat to her "self-esteem." The fact that her anger is directed toward the other person serves the purpose of protecting her own shaky self-esteem.

Discomfort disturbance, on the other hand, is more closely related to the domain of human comfort and occurs when we hold rigid beliefs about comfort and comfortable life conditions and demand that they must exist. Ego and discomfort disturbance are not discrete categories but can frequently overlap, as when, for example, a client berates himself as weak (ego disturbance) for being unable to cope with a stressful work environment (discomfort disturbance). The rational solution to ego disturbance is to strive for unconditional self-acceptance; for discomfort disturbance, it is to acquire a philosophy of discomfort tolerance.

THEORY OF CHANGE IN REBT

Given that we are not slaves to our tendency to think irrationally, REBT argues that we can change, particularly if we internalize three major insights:

1. Past or present adversities do not "cause" our disturbed emotional and behavioral consequences. Rather, our disturbed feelings and behaviors are largely created by our rigid and extreme irrational beliefs about these adversities.

2. Irrespective of how we have disturbed ourselves in the past, we remain disturbed chiefly because we maintain our conviction in our irrational beliefs and act and think in ways that are consistent with them. When we do so, such behavior and thinking serve to reinforce our irrational beliefs.

3. Because we are human and very easily (and to some degree, naturally) tend to disturb ourselves, and because we find it easy to cling to our self-defeating irrational beliefs and associated feelings and actions, we can, albeit with difficulty, overcome our disturbances in the long run, but only by working hard and repeatedly questioning our irrational beliefs and the effects of these beliefs.

Part II

PRACTICE

OVERVIEW OF REBT PRACTICE

REBT is a structured approach to emotional problem solving in which the therapist adopts an active-directive approach to helping clients solve their own problems. REBT is multimodal in nature in that therapists use and encourage their clients to use a variety of cognitive, imaginal, behavioral, and emotive-evocative techniques to facilitate therapeutic change. Rational emotive behavior therapists consider that the bulk of therapeutic change is achieved by clients in their daily lives rather than inside therapy sessions. Therefore, therapists routinely encourage their clients to carry out homework assignments that are individually designed to help them put into practice what they have learned within therapy sessions.

The following discussion provides a brief overview of the basic REBT treatment process, as summarized in Table 1. For the purpose of illustration, we assume that you will be dealing with your client's emotional problems one at a time. We thus restrict ourselves to specifying the treatment process as it pertains to a given client problem.

TABLE 1   The Rational Emotive Behavioral Treatment Sequence

Step 1: Ask for a Problem

Step 2: Clarify and Select the Target Problem

Step 3: Formulate the Target Problem

Step 4: Set a Goal with Respect to the Formulated Problem

Step 5: Ask for a Specific Example of the Target Problem

Step 6: Assess the Situation

Step 7: Assess C

Step 8: Assess A

Step 9: Agree upon a Goal with Respect to the Assessed Problem

Step 10: Help Your Client to See the Link between the Formulated Problem Goal and the Assessed Problem Goal

Step 11: Identify and Assess Any Meta-emotional Problems If Relevant

Step 12: Teach the B–C Connection

Step 13: Assess iB

Step 14: Connect iB and the Emotional Problem and rB and the Emotional Goal

Step 15: Question iB and rB

Step 16: Prepare Your Client to Deepen Conviction in Rational Beliefs

Step 17: Check the Validity of A

Step 18: Negotiate a Homework Assignment

Step 19: Check Homework Assignments

Step 20: Facilitate the Working-through Process

Note: A = adversity; B = belief; iB = irrational belief; rB = rational belief; C = consequence of irrational belief

Once again, it is important to point out that the actual clinical situation may be far more complex than is indicated in this brief analysis.

Before beginning the treatment process outlined in the following pages, it is important first to greet the client and settle any practical issues that may be of concern (e.g., fees and scheduling of appointments).

Step 1 | Ask for a Problem

After you discuss the necessary practicalities, we suggest that you establish the problem-solving orientation of REBT immediately by asking your client what problem she would like to discuss first. Once selected, this problem is known as the target problem. Establishing the target problem communicates a number of messages to the client. First, it emphasizes that you are both there to get a job done (i.e., to help the client overcome her emotional problems). Second, it illustrates that REBT is an efficient and focused approach to emotional problem solving. Third, it indicates that, as a therapist, you are going to be active and direct your client immediately to a discussion of her problems.

Client's choice versus client's most serious problem

You can adopt two basic strategies when asking your client to focus on a target problem. In the first case, you ask your client to choose the issue ("What would you like to work on first?"). The client's selection may or may not be her most serious problem. In the second case, you ask your client to start with her most serious problem ("What are you most bothered about in your life right now?").

When your client does not identify a target problem

What can you do if your client does not identify a target problem? (This situation often arises when your "client" is a fellow mental health practitioner with whom you are conducting a peer counseling session during REBT training.) First, let your client know that she does not have to choose a serious problem. Tell her that it is perfect-ly in order to start the process with an issue that is impeding her in some slight way. Remind her that there is always something to work on because human beings usually operate at a less than optimal level of functioning. Encourage your client to identify feelings or behaviors she would like to decrease or increase. If this fails, ask your client if she procrastinates. Very few of us don't, and this problem could then be agreed on as your client's target problem.

Another, more indirect, way of helping your client disclose a tar-get problem is to ask what she would like to achieve from therapy. When your client articulates a goal, you could then ask for ways in which she is currently not achieving this goal. This approach may well lead to a discussion of feelings and/or behaviors that your client identifies as impediments. You could then explore these impediments further without necessarily labeling them problems. The word *problem* serves to discourage some clients from becoming engaged in a problem-focused therapy such as REBT. If this is the case, use a term that is more acceptable (e.g., difficulties, challenges).

Step 2 | Clarify and Select the Target Problem

The nature of your client's problem may be obvious after an initial discussion. If this is the case, you may proceed to formulate the problem (Step 3) or to assess a specific example of it (Steps 6 through 10). However, when your client's target problem is unclear, or when she has disclosed a number of problems, the two of you should work to clarify the problem in the first case and select the problem you are going to work on first in the second case (i.e., the target problem).

Arriving at a common understanding of the problem and agreeing to work on it is an important therapeutic ingredient in REBT in that it strengthens the therapeutic alliance (Dryden, 2006). Doing so enables you and your client to work as a team and helps your client to feel understood and have confidence that you know what you are doing.

When you clarify and select a target problem with your client, there are a number of issues that you need to bear in mind.

Distinguish between an emotional and a practical problem

As Bard (1980) has noted, REBT is a method of psychotherapy that helps clients overcome their emotional problems and not their practical problems. Of course, clients often have emotional problems about their practical problems, and these may well become the focus of therapeutic exploration. Also, as clients' emotional problems (e.g., anxiety) are addressed, their practical problems (e.g., lack of finances) may also be solved, even though the therapeutic exploration does not expressly deal with such issues (Ellis, 2002). In any case, it is important to help your client to understand this distinction.

Target unhealthy, not healthy negative emotions

In Part I of this primer, we distinguished between unhealthy and healthy negative emotions. Do not encourage your client to change HNE's, as these healthy reactions to adversities will help your client to (a) adjust constructively to an adversity if it can't be changed or (b) change the adversity if it can be changed. However, do target for change UNE's (i.e., those that stem from irrational beliefs). Help your client to understand the difference between these two types of negative emotions (see Appendix 1). The question "How is this a problem for you?" will often lead to a useful discussion and will help you and your client to identify and define a "real" emotional problem.

Operationalize vague problems

When your client discusses her target problem in vague or confusing terms, it is important that you help her to operationalize the problem. For example, if your client says, "My husband is a pain in the ass," help her to specify what this statement means in operational terms (e.g., "What is it your husband does that leads you to conclude that he is a pain in the ass, and how do you feel when he acts this way?").

If you do this, you will find that you are beginning to formulate the problem in ABC terms. The adversity (A) is the husband's behavior that makes him "a pain in the ass"; the emotional problem (C) is the disturbed, unhealthy emotion (e.g., problematic anger) your client feels when her husband acts badly.

Focus on helping your client change C, not the adversity at A

A common difficulty you may face at this point is that your client may wish to change the adversity at A rather than her feelings (C) about it. As noted earlier, changing the adversity is a practical solution; changing the C is the emotional solution. If you encounter this difficulty, you can use a number of strategies to encourage your client to change C before attempting to change A:

1. You can help your client to see that she can change A more effectively if she is not emotionally disturbed about it at C.

2. It may be that your client already knows how to change A but cannot do so at this time. If this is the case, it is important to help her

understand that the reason she cannot use her productive problem-solving strategies to change A is that she probably is emotionally disturbed about A.

3. If your client does not yet have productive problem-solving strategies in her repertoire to change A, you can often encourage her to focus on her problems at C by showing her that she will learn such strategies more effectively if she is not emotionally disturbed about A.

When you still have not identified a problem

If at this stage you still have not reached an agreement with your client concerning the nature of the problem, you can suggest that she keep a problem diary. Encourage your client to monitor her disturbed feelings during the following week and suggest that she make written notes of what these feelings are, as well as when and where she experiences them.

Step 3 | Formulate the Target Problem

When you help your client to formulate her target problem, you have a clear statement of this problem informed by the Situational ABC framework that we discussed in Part I of the primer.

We suggest that you use the following points in formulating your client's target problem:

1. [Situations] – Help your client to identify the situations in which she experiences her problem.

2. [A] – Help your client to identify the theme of the target problem. Ask her what is it about the situations that she specified that is a problem for her. This is likely to be an inference. Consult Appendix 1 for help on this point.

3. [C (Emotional)] – Help your client to identify the one major UNE that she experiences when she encounters the situations and theme that she specified. This will be one of the following: anxiety, depression, guilt, shame, hurt, problematic anger, problematic jealousy, and problematic envy.

4. [C (Behavioral)] – Help your client to identify the dysfunctional behavior that she demonstrated in these situations. Remember that this might be an overt action or an action tendency.

5. [C (Cognitive)] – If relevant, help your client to identify the thinking that she engaged in once her UNE "kicked in."

Here is an example.

1. Type of situation: Whenever I have a medical symptom that I can't explain [Situations]

2. Theme: I don't know whether the symptom is benign [A]

3. Major UNE: Anxiety [C (Emotional)]

4. Behavior: I seek reassurance that the symptom is benign [C (Behavioral)]

5. Thinking: I am seriously ill [C (Cognitive)]

Putting this into a sentence, we have the client's formulated problem.

> *Whenever I have a medical symptom that I can't explain, I feel anxious about not knowing whether the symptom is benign and seek reassurance that it is benign. Despite this, I think that I am seriously ill.*

<table>
<tr><td>Step 4</td><td># Set a Goal with Respect to the Formulated Problem</td></tr>
</table>

It is useful at this point to help your client to set a goal with respect to his formulated target problem. Doing so gives REBT a sense of direction and helps your client to see that change is possible, which engenders a sense of hope and increases his motivation to engage in the process of REBT.

We again suggest that you use the following points in helping your client to set a goal with respect to his formulated target emotional problem.

1. [Situations] – Help your client to identify the situations in which he experiences his problem. This will be the same as he specified in his formulated target problem.

2. [A] – Help your client to identify the theme of the problem. This will again be the same as your client specified in his formulated target problem.

3. [C (Emotional Goal)] – Help your client to identify the healthy alternative to the major UNE that he experiences when he encounters the situations and theme that he specified earlier. Note that this emotional goal should be negative because it is about an adversity, but it should also be healthy in the sense that it will enable your client to deal effectively with the adversity if it can be changed or to adjust constructively to it if it cannot be changed. This will be one of the following: concern (as opposed to anxiety), sadness (as opposed to depression), remorse (as opposed to guilt), disappointment (as opposed to shame), sorrow (as opposed to hurt), nonproblematic anger (as opposed to problematic anger),

nonproblematic jealousy (as opposed to problematic jealousy), and nonproblematic envy (as opposed to problematic envy).

4. [C (Behavioral Goal)] – Help your client to identify the functional alternative to the unconstructive behavior that he demonstrated in his formulated target problem. Again, this might be an overt action or an action tendency.

5. [C (Cognitive Goal)] – If relevant, help your client to identify the realistic alternative to the distorted thinking that he has engaged in.

Note that when you help your client to set a goal for his formulated target problem, he is only changing his emotional, behavioral, and thinking responses to the situations and the theme in these situations that he finds problematic. The reason is that in REBT we want the client to be prepared to face life's adversities even when these may not occur.

Here are the goals set by the person whose emotional problem was formulated in Step 3. As noted in the preceding list, the first two points are the same in the goal section as in the formulated problem section.

1. Type of situation: Whenever I have a medical symptom that I can't explain [Situations]

2. Theme: I don't know whether the symptom is benign [A]

3. Major HNE: Concern (rather than anxiety) [C (Emotional Goal)]

4. Behavior: To get on with everyday tasks (rather than seek reassurance that the symptom is benign) [C (Behavioral Goal)]

5. Thinking: To think that, although I may be seriously ill, I am more likely to be okay, without having to reassure myself (rather than to think that I am seriously ill) [C (Cognitive Goal)]

Putting this into a sentence, we have the client's goal with respect to her formulated target problem:

> *Whenever I have a medical symptom that I can't explain, I want to feel concerned rather than anxious about not knowing that the symptom is benign. I want to get on with everyday tasks rather than seek reassurance that my symptom is benign, and I want to think that, although I may be seriously ill, I am more likely to be okay, without*

having to reassure myself (rather than to think that I am
seriously ill).

Note that under the headings of "emotional goal," "behavioral goal," and "cognitive goal," we suggest that you encourage your client to use the "rather than" wording to highlight the difference between her problem response and her goal response. However, if she finds doing this cumbersome, then encourage her to omit the "rather than" phrases.

One last point: When discussing goal selection with your client, keep in mind the distinction between long-term goals and short-term goals. Your client may choose a short-term goal that may in the long term be self-defeating and therefore irrational (e.g., in the case of an anorexic client, the desire to lose more weight). Therefore, encourage your client to take a longer-term perspective when choosing goals for change and to make a commitment to carrying out the hard work to achieve them.

| **Step 5** | Ask for a Specific Example of the Target Problem |

In clarifying and selecting a target problem with your client, it is important that you be as specific as you can. Because your client experiences his emotional problems and holds related irrational beliefs in specific contexts, being specific will help you to obtain reliable and valid data about the situation and about A, B, and C. Giving your client a plausible rationale for specificity is a good idea, especially if he tends to discuss his target problems in vague terms. Help him to understand that being specific about the problem will help him deal more constructively with it in the situations about which he is disturbed. A good way of modeling specificity for your client is to ask for a recent or typical example of the target problem (e.g., "When was the last time you experienced this problem?").

If, after repeated attempts, your client is still unable to provide you with a specific example of the target problem, this may be evidence that he has a meta-emotional problem (e.g., shame) about his original emotional problem (e.g., anxiety). If you suspect this is the case, do not assume that you are correct: Test your hypothesis. (See Step 11 for further discussion of this point.)

Step 6 | Assess the Situation

If you have played the game Clue (known as Cluedo in Britain), you will know that a murder has been committed and that the purpose of the game is to guess the identity of the murderer, how he or she committed the murder, and where the crime was committed. The game assumes that a specific event has happened, and you have to stipulate the descriptive elements of the situation in which the event occurred. The same holds when you help your client to describe the situation in which the specific example of her problem occurred.

Imagine that your client's target problem centers on her feeling anxious in the presence of authority figures. You have asked her to select a specific example of her problem, and she chooses the last time this happened. Here is how to assess the situation:

You: Where were you when you felt anxious?

Client: I was in the staff meeting in my boss's office.

You: Who was there?

Client: Me, my boss, and my two colleagues.

You: When did you start to feel anxious?

Client: Just before the item when I was going to speak.

You: So to sum up: You felt anxious in the staff meeting with your boss and your two colleagues, particularly just before the item on which you were going to speak.

Client: Exactly.

You will note that all these elements can be verified and do not contain any client inferences that would go beyond the data at hand.

The main purpose of assessing the situation is to provide a descriptive context to which you can refer throughout the assessment and therapy process when dealing with this specific example. It aids your client's memory, in the preceding example, of her anxious response and the important factors that make up her anxiety, and this memory will help her to provide the ABC that you are looking to work with.

Avoid pitfalls in assessing the situation

1. Discourage your client from describing the situation in which the problem occurred in vague terms. Get as clear and specific an example of a situation as you can. (An example of a vague situation would be the statement "My wife reacted negatively to me." In contrast, a specific situation would be "My wife called me a jerk when I told her I cried at the movie last night.")

2. Discourage your client from talking about several situations at one time. In REBT, it is important for you to work on one situation at a time; therefore, encourage your client to deal with the situation he considers to best illustrate the context in which he makes himself disturbed.

Step 7 | Assess C

At this stage, although you may assess C or A, depending on which element of the specific example of her target problem your client raises first, we suggest that you start with assessing C because the UNE that you identify will then provide clues to the theme of your client's A (see Appendix 1). We will, therefore, begin by considering issues involved in the assessment of C.

Check again for an unhealthy negative emotion

In assessing C, remember that your client's emotional problem will be an unhealthy (disturbed) negative emotion, not a healthy (undisturbed) negative emotion. As noted earlier, a UNE differs from an HNE in that the former usually involves a great deal of emotional pain, motivates one to behave in a self-defeating manner, blocks one from achieving one's goals, and leads to unrealistic thinking.

Appendix 1 lists words used in REBT theory to distinguish between these two types of negative emotions. Although these distinctions are important, you should not necessarily expect your client to use this terminology in the same way that you do. For example, she may talk about anxiety when she is actually experiencing concern, or vice versa (Dryden, 1986). It is important that you identify a UNE and that you and your client use the same language when referring to it. You may either encourage your client to adopt the REBT terminology of emotion, or you may choose to adopt his or her use of feeling language. Whatever course you take, be consistent in your vocabulary throughout therapy.

Focus on an emotional C

We recognize that C may be emotional, behavioral, or cognitive. If your client identifies or discusses a behavioral or cognitive C, then look for the emotional C that is associated with the behavioral or cognitive C. For example, dysfunctional behaviors are often defensive in nature and exist to help clients avoid experiencing certain UNE's; therefore, encourage your client to avoid dealing with dysfunctional behaviors and focus instead on UNE's. Thus, if your client wishes to stop smoking, regard smoking as a defensive behavior and encourage him to identify the problematic emotions he might experience were he to refrain from smoking. We suggest that you also adopt this strategy if your client identifies his problem as procrastination or some other kind of avoidance behavior.

Clarify the emotional C

If your client identifies a vague emotional C, there are a number of specific techniques you can use to clarify its nature. For example, you can use imagery methods or Gestalt exercises, such as the empty-chair technique (Passons, 1975) or Gendlin's (1978) focusing technique. When Ellis's clients experienced difficulty in identifying a specific emotion, he used to encourage them to "Take a wild guess," a method that yielded surprisingly useful information about their emotional C's.

Understand that frustration is an A, not a C

Your client may talk about feeling frustrated at C. Some REBT therapists consider frustration to be an adversity at A rather than a feeling at C (Trexler, 1976). As a C, frustration in REBT theory is usually regarded as an HNE experienced by your client when his goals are blocked. However, when your client says that he feels frustrated, it is possible that he is referring to a UNE. One way of telling whether your client's frustration is a healthy or an unhealthy negative emotion is to ask him if the feeling is bearable. If your client says the feeling is unbearable, then it may well be that he is experiencing a UNE (e.g., rage) that should be targeted for change. Another way of distinguishing healthy from unhealthy frustration as a feeling is to ask your client how he acted or felt like acting when he "felt" frustrated. If his behavior was constructive, then your client's "feeling" of frustration was likely to be healthy; whereas, if his behavior was unconstructive, then the frustration that he "felt" was probably unhealthy.

Avoid pitfalls in assessing C

There are a number of pitfalls in assessing your client's problematic emotions at C. The following suggestions will help you avoid them:

1. Do not ask questions that reinforce the assumption that A causes C. Novice REBT therapists frequently ask their clients, "How did that make you feel?" An alternative question that does not imply that A causes C is "How did you feel about that?"

2. Do not accept vague descriptions of feelings such as "bad," "upset," "miserable," and so forth. When your client uses vague terms, help her to clarify exactly what she feels at C. (See Appendix 1 for discriminations among negative emotions, and also see Crawford & Ellis, 1989). Also, do not accept statements such as "I feel trapped" or "I feel rejected" as descriptions of emotions occurring at C. Recognize that we do not have a feeling called trapped or rejected. These terms usually refer to A's and sometimes to combinations of A, B, and C factors. In the latter case, it is important to distinguish among these three and to ensure that your client's C statements actually do refer to emotions. In the former case, if your client says, "I feel rejected," for example, help her to recognize that she may have been rejected at A. Then ask how she felt at point C about the rejection at A (e.g., "hurt," "ashamed").

Step 8 | Assess A

If you have chosen first to assess C, your next step will be to assess A. As noted earlier, A refers to an adversity. This may be an actual adversity that may be regarded as confirmable reality (i.e., your client's view of the adversity can be confirmed as accurate by neutral observers). However, in this book, A more often stands for your client's personally significant inferences or interpretations about what happened in the situation.

Be specific in assessing A

As with assessments of C, it is important for you to be as specific as you can when you assess A in your client's specific example of his target problem. Thus you may be considering the last time A occurred, a typical example of A, or the most relevant example of A your client can recall.

Remember that A is the inference the client makes about the situation that triggers B

While you are assessing A, it is important for you to remember that A is the most relevant part of the situation that triggered your client's irrational belief at B, which, in turn, largely determined his UNE at C.

Here are some tips concerning how best to identify your client's A.

1. Focus on the "situation" that your client has described.
2. Ask him what one thing would get rid of or significantly diminish the UNE that he felt at C.

3. The opposite of this is your client's A.

   Here is an example of using these three points in identifying the A. Your client's described "situation" is: "My boss asked to see me at the end of the day," and her emotional C is anxiety.

   1. Focus your client's attention on the "situation" that she described: "My boss asked to see me at the end of the day."

   2. Ask her what one thing would get rid of or significantly diminish the anxiety that she felt at C: "My boss not getting cross with me."

   3. The opposite of this is your client's A: "My boss getting cross with me."

Encourage your client to assume temporarily that A is true

When you assess A, you may discover that your client's A is a clear distortion of reality. If this is the case, you may be tempted to question A. Resist this temptation. Rather, at this stage you should encourage your client to assume temporarily that A is correct. For example, in the case previously described, it is not important to determine whether your client's boss would have been cross with her. What is important is that you encourage your client to assume that A is correct in order to help her to identify more accurately the irrational beliefs about the A that led to her feelings at C. Later in the treatment sequence (at Step 17), you will have an opportunity to check as to whether A is likely to have been true.

Avoid pitfalls in assessing A

There are a number of pitfalls in assessing A. The following suggestions can help you to avoid them.

1. Do not obtain too much detail about the situation in which the client's A is embedded. Allowing your client to talk at length about the situation can discourage you both from retaining a problem-solving approach to overcoming emotional difficulties. If your client does provide too much detail, try to abstract the salient theme or summarize what you understand to be her A. Interrupt your client tactfully and reestablish an REBT-driven

assessment focus if she does begin to discuss the situation at length. For example, you could say, "I think you may be giving me more detail than I require. What was it about the situation that you were most disturbed about?"

2. Do not assume that the first inference that your client comes up with is her A. Ask for other inferences that she might have made in the situation, then apply the technique described in the earlier section ("Remember that A is the inference the client makes about the situation that triggers B) to identify your client's A.

3. Do not accept an A unless it reflects the theme associated with the UNE you have already assessed. Consult Appendix 1 for information about inferential themes associated with the eight emotional problems for which clients typically seek help.

When you still have not identified A

If at this stage your client has still not identified a clear A, encourage her to keep a diary during the time before her next session. In this diary, she can record examples of situations in which she made herself disturbed. These can be used to identify the inferential theme of this disturbance, and you can then work with a specific example of this theme.

| **Step 9** | Agree upon a Goal with Respect to the Assessed Problem |

Once you have assessed the A and C elements of your client's specific example of his or her target problem, you may find that the assessed problem is different from the formulated problem (Step 3). For example, let's say that your client's formulated problem is being overweight and that she states that her goal is to achieve and maintain a specific target weight. However, when a specific example of her overeating is assessed, you discover that she becomes anxious and overeats when she is bored. At this point, your client's goal with respect to the assessed problem would involve dealing more constructively with the feeling of boredom so that she does not use the counterproductive strategy of overeating. Thus you may encourage your client to feel concerned (rather than anxious) about being bored and to use that feeling of concern to deal with boredom in more constructive ways, such as studying. You can use the Situational ABC framework to do this, as shown in Tables 2 and 3. Note again that C is the only component of the framework to change here (see Step 4 also).

So, at the assessment stage, encourage your client to select as a goal a healthy negative emotion (HNE) and help her to understand why such an emotion is a realistic and constructive response to the adversity at A.

Consider your client's motivation to change C

Sometimes a client will experience a UNE that he is not motivated to change. This lack of motivation can result when your client does not recognize the destructive nature of the emotion he is experiencing.

45

TABLE 2   Assessed Problem

Situation	A	B	C
Not having anything to do	Bored	Yet to be assessed	Emotional: Anxiety Behavioral: Overeating

TABLE 3   Goal with Respect to the Assessed Problem

Situation	A	B	C
Not having anything to do	Bored	Yet to be assessed	Emotional: Concern (rather than anxiety) Behavioral: Studying (rather than overeating)

This situation occurs most frequently in the case of anger; it also sometimes happens in the cases of guilt and depression. We therefore recommend that you assess your client's understanding of the dysfunctionality or self-defeating nature of the target emotion (C). This process can begin at Step 7, but it is more important when identifying your client's goal in relation to the assessed problem. If your client does not understand why his emotion is unhealthy, spend as much time as necessary helping him to understand this point. Basically, this can be accomplished in three steps:

1. Help your client to assess the consequences of the UNE. What happens when he feels this way? Does he act constructively? Does he act self-defeatingly? Does he stop himself from acting appropriately?

2. Point out that the goal is to replace the UNE with the corresponding HNE. Getting this point across may be difficult, especially if your client has rigid ideas about the ways he is supposed to feel.

However, if provided with appropriate models, your client will usually be able to understand that one can experience the healthy emotion in any given situation.

3. Finally, assess what the consequences would be if your client felt the corresponding healthy emotion in the same situation. Because he has probably not considered such a change, help him to imagine how he would act and how the outcome would be different if he did experience the healthy emotion in the context of the adversity. Compare the outcomes of both healthy and unhealthy negative emotions. Your client will usually understand the advantages of the healthy emotion, and this will increase his motivation to change C.

Avoid pitfalls when agreeing upon goals with respect to the assessed problem

Several pitfalls need to be avoided when agreeing upon goals after the client's problem has been assessed. The following suggestions will be helpful in doing so:

1. Do not accept your client's goal statements when she expresses the wish to experience less of a UNE (e.g., "I want to feel less anxious" or "I want to feel less guilty"). According to rational emotive behavioral theory, the presence of a UNE (e.g., anxiety or guilt) in such statements indicates that your client is still holding an irrational belief, albeit in a less intense manner. Thus we advise you to help your client distinguish between the UNE and its healthy negative counterpart. Encourage your client to set the latter emotion as her goal. She can therefore choose to feel concerned instead of anxious and remorseful instead of guilty, for example.

2. Do not accept goals that indicate that your client wishes to feel neutral, indifferent, or calm toward aversive events about which it would be rational to feel HNE's (e.g., disappointment). Emotions indicating indifference (e.g., calmness when an unfortunate event occurs) mean that your client does not have a rational belief about the event in question and that, in reality, she probably would prefer that the event had not happened. If you go along with your client's goal to feel calm or indifferent about a negative event, you will encourage her to deny the existence of her desires rather than to think rationally.

3. For similar reasons, do not accept your client's goal to experience positive feelings about an adversity at A. It is unrealistic for your client to feel happy, for example, when she is faced with a negative life event that she would prefer not to encounter (e.g., a loss or failure). If you accept your client's goal to feel positive about an adversity, you will encourage her to believe that it is good that this adversity occurred. By doing this, you will once again be discouraging your client from thinking rationally. To reiterate an earlier point, when you encourage your client to experience HNE's in the face of unpleasant life events, you help her to come to terms with or to change her situation.

4. Finally, do not accept vague goals (e.g., "I want to be happy"). The more specific you can encourage your client to be in setting goals (e.g., "What specific things would you like to achieve in your life that will help to make you happy?"), the more likely it is that she will be motivated to do the hard work of changing her irrational beliefs in the service of achieving these goals.

Step 10	Help Your Client to See the Link between the Formulated Problem Goal and the Assessed Problem Goal

Because there have been two goal-setting stages (Steps 4 and 9), your client may become confused as to how different goals have emerged. Of course, the goals may be the same if the problems have remained the same at Steps 4 and 9. If the former is the case, do not assume that your client will automatically see the link between these two goal-setting stages, but help him to understand that the assessed goal is based on a more detailed understanding of his problems than was attempted at Step 4.

| **Step 11** | Identify and Assess Any Meta-emotional Problems If Relevant |

Clients frequently have meta-emotional problems about their original emotional problems (e.g., anger about feeling depressed). A meta-emotional problem is literally an emotional problem that your client has about his or her emotional problem. Another way of stating this step is as follows: Does the client have secondary emotional problems about his or her primary emotional problems? If your client's original problem is anxiety, you may ask, "How do you feel about feeling anxious?" to determine whether your client does in fact have a meta-emotional problem about his or her original problem of anxiety.

Know when to work on the meta-emotional problem first

If any of the following three conditions are met, we suggest that you first focus attention on your client's meta-emotional problem.

1. Your client's meta-emotional problem interferes significantly with the work you are trying to do on her original problem. Such interference might take place either in the session or in the client's outside life.

2. From a clinical perspective, the meta-emotional problem is the more important of the two. You will learn to identify when this is the case through supervision and with greater clinical experience.

3. Your client can see the sense of working on her meta-emotional problem first.

You may need to present a plausible rationale for starting with the meta-emotional problem first. If, after you have presented your rationale, your client still wishes to work on her original problem first, then do so. To do otherwise may threaten the productive therapeutic alliance you have by now established.

Check for an emotional problem about a healthy negative emotion

When you have assessed a specific example of your client's formulated problem, you may decide that she is, in fact, experiencing an HNE (e.g., sadness in response to an important loss). If so, check to see whether your client has an emotional problem with this healthy emotion. For example, your client may feel ashamed about feeling sad. If this is the case, work to reach an agreement that the meta-emotional problem (shame) will be the client's target problem and then carry out a Situational ABC assessment of this agreed-upon problem.

Assess the presence of shame

As noted earlier, if your client is reluctant to disclose that she has an emotional problem, she may feel ashamed about having the problem or about disclosing it to a therapist. When you suspect that this might be the case, ask your client how she would feel if she did have an emotional problem about the adversity that you are discussing. If the client says she would feel ashamed, agree with her to work on shame as the target problem before encouraging her to disclose the original problem she had in mind.

Step 12 | Teach the B–C Connection

By now you will have assessed the A and C elements of the specific example of your client's original problem or metaproblem. The next step is to teach the B–C connection—the notion that your client's emotional problem is determined largely by his beliefs at B rather than by the adversity at A that you have already assessed. Carrying out this step is critical. Unless your client understands that his emotional problem is determined by his beliefs, he will not understand why you want to assess his beliefs during the next step of the treatment process. Using an example unrelated to your client's problem can often help to explain the concept. Other exercises and metaphors to help teach the idea are detailed in the REBT texts listed in the reference section of this book (e.g., Ellis & Dryden, 1997; Walen et al., 1992).

Step 13 | Assess iB

While assessing B, keep in mind the distinction between your client's rational beliefs (rB) and irrational beliefs (iB), and help her to understand the difference between these two kinds of thinking.

Assess both premise and derivative forms

In Part I of this primer, we argued that your client's beliefs can be divided into a premise and certain derivatives from this premise. At this stage of the process, you should carefully assess your client's irrational beliefs. As you do so, assess both the premise form (rigid beliefs such as dogmatic musts, absolute shoulds, have-tos, oughts, etc.) and the three main derivatives from the premise: (1) awfulizing beliefs, (2) discomfort-intolerance beliefs, and (3) depreciation beliefs (of self, others, and/or life conditions). As you do this, you can either teach and use the REBT terms for these processes or use your client's own language, ensuring that her terms accurately reflect irrational beliefs. Base your decision on your client's feedback concerning which of these strategies will be the most useful to her.

Remember the three basic rigid beliefs

While assessing your client's irrational beliefs, keep in mind the three basic rigid beliefs outlined in Part I: demands about self, demands about others, and demands about world/life conditions.

Distinguish between absolute shoulds and other shoulds

While you are assessing the premise form of your client's irrational beliefs, your client may use the word *should*. This word has several

55

different meanings in the English language. Most expressions of the word *should* are unrelated to your client's emotional problems. These include shoulds of preference ("You should preferably treat your children with respect"); empirical shoulds ("When two parts of hydrogen and one part of oxygen are mixed, you should get water"); and shoulds of recommendation ("You should go and see that excellent play at the local theater"). Rational emotive behavioral theory hypothesizes that only absolute shoulds are related to emotional disturbance. If your client finds the different meanings confusing, it may be helpful to substitute the word *must* in cases in which an irrational belief in its premise form may be operative. (Compare, for instance, "I should be admired by my colleagues" with "I must be admired by my colleagues.") It is Ellis's and our clinical experience that the word *must* conveys the meaning of rigidity better than the word *should*. In particular, help your client to distinguish between absolute shoulds and shoulds of preference.

Use questions in assessing irrational beliefs

When you assess your client's irrational beliefs, use questions. A standard question that REBT therapists frequently ask is "What were you telling yourself about A to make yourself disturbed at C?" This type of open-ended question has both advantages and disadvantages. The main advantage in using this type of inquiry is that you are unlikely to put words in your client's mouth concerning the content of her belief. The main disadvantage is that your client will be unlikely to respond by articulating an irrational belief. Rather, she is most likely to give you further inferences at A—ones that may well be less relevant than the one you pinpointed at Step 8.

Imagine, for example, that your client is particularly anxious that other people will think her a fool if she stammers in public. Asking her "What were you telling yourself about other people's criticism to make yourself disturbed at C?" might yield the response "I thought they wouldn't like me." Note that this thought is in fact an inference and that you still do not know what your client's irrational belief is. In this instance, you want to help the client to understand that her statement does not describe an irrational belief; you also want to educate her to look further for her irrational belief about A. You can do this by judiciously combining the use of open-ended questions with some didactic explanation.

What other kinds of open-ended questions can you use when assessing your client's irrational beliefs? Walen et al. (1992) list a number of possibilities, such as "What was going through your mind?" "Were you aware of any thoughts in your head?" "What was on your mind then?" and "Are you aware of what you were thinking at that moment?" Again, note that your client may not spontaneously come up (and, in our experience, probably won't come up) with irrational beliefs in response to these questions; she may well need further help of a didactic nature.

An alternative to asking open-ended questions is to ask theory-driven questions (i.e., questions that are directly derived from rational emotive behavioral theory). For example, to elicit an answer specifying a rigid belief (i.e., a premise), you might ask, "What demand were you making about other people's criticism to make yourself disturbed at point C?" To assess the presence of a derivative of a rigid belief, you might ask, "What kind of person did you think you were for stammering and incurring other people's criticism?"

The advantage of theory-driven questions is that they orient your client to look for her irrational beliefs. The danger is that you may be putting words in your client's mouth and encouraging her to look for irrational beliefs that she may not have. However, you will minimize this danger if you have already established that your client has a UNE at point C.

Use the choice-based assessment technique to identify iB

One of us (W. D.) has invented an assessment technique to identify a client's iB that is particularly effective. I (W. D.) call this the choice-based assessment technique.

We present an example of how to use this method in identifying the client's premise and provide a commentary on the thinking that underpins the therapist's interventions. We then outline, in more general terms, the points to follow with your clients when using this technique. Please note that similar progressive points can be used in assessing your client's derivative beliefs.

In this example, the client's boss has asked to see her (Situation), and she is anxious (C) in case he is cross with her (A). The therapist has made the B–C connection and is working with the client to identify her premise belief.

Therapist: Now we know that it is important to you that your boss is not cross with you. Is that right?

Here the therapist asserts the client's preference. This underpins both her rigid belief and her nondogmatic preference; see Part I.

Client: Yes, that's correct.

Therapist: Okay. I will now outline two beliefs that you could have been holding at the time. Can I outline them and then you can tell me which belief underpinned your anxiety?

Here the therapist is drawing on REBT theory and thus is using a theory-derived method of inquiry.

Client: Okay.

Therapist: At the time when you were anxious, was your anxiety based on belief number 1: "It's important to me that my boss is not cross with me, and therefore he must not be cross with me," or belief number 2: "It's important to me that my boss is not cross with me, but that does not mean that he must not be cross with me"?

Client: Definitely belief number 1.

How to use the choice-based assessment technique to identify iB

1. Assert the client's preference about A and elicit client agreement.
2. State that the client could hold one of two beliefs that account for his or her emotional C and ask for permission to present them.
3. State the client's C and then present the two beliefs (rigid belief and nondogmatic preference; see Part I).
4. Ask the client which belief accounted for his or her C.

| **Step 14** | Connect iB and the Emotional Problem and rB and the Emotional Goal |

After you have accurately assessed your client's irrational beliefs in the form of both premise and derivatives, ensure that your client understands the connection between her irrational belief (iB) and her disturbed emotion at point C before proceeding to question the iB. Thus you might ask, "Can you understand that, as long as you demand that other people must not criticize you, you are bound to make yourself anxious about this happening?" or "Can you see that, as long as you believe that you are no good for being regarded by others as a fool, you will be anxious about being criticized?" If your client says "yes," you can then capitalize on this and prepare the ground for disputing the irrational belief (e.g., "So, in order to change your feeling of anxiety to one of concern, what do you need to change first?")

Eliciting the connection between irrational beliefs and disturbed emotions is likely to be more productive than telling your client that such a connection exists. If your client says that she understands that she needs to change her belief in order to change her feeling, this will indicate that she has grasped the concept. If she does not see the connection, spend time helping her to understand it before beginning to dispute her irrational beliefs.

If possible, at this juncture, you should also look for ways of helping your client to understand the connection between her rational belief and her emotional goal. Using the choice-based assessment technique to identify iB helps you to do just this. Let us demonstrate this by revisiting the dialogue presented in Step 13.

Therapist: Now we know that it is important to you that your boss is not cross with you. Is that right?

Client: Yes, that's correct.

Therapist: Okay. I will now outline two beliefs that you could have been holding at the time. Can I outline them and then you can tell me which belief underpinned your anxiety?

Client: Okay.

Therapist: At the time when you were anxious, was your anxiety based on belief number 1: "It's important to me that my boss is not cross with me, and therefore he must not be cross with me," or belief number 2: "It's important to me that my boss is not cross with me, but that does not mean that he must not be cross with me"?

Client: Definitely belief number 1.

Therapist: So if you believe that that your boss must not be cross with you, then you will feel . . . ?

The therapist is encouraging the client to make the iB–emotional problem connection.

Client: Anxious.

The client shows that she understands this connection.

Therapist: How would you feel about the possibility of your boss being cross with you if you hold belief number 2— namely, that you would not want him to be cross with you, but that that does not mean that he must not be cross with you?

Here the therapist is asking to see if the client will come up with the rB–healthy emotion connection.

Client: Well, I guess I would be concerned . . .

Therapist: Rather than anxious?

Client: Yes.

The client understands this new healthier connection.

Therapist: Which, if you recall, was your stated goal about how to respond to negativity from your boss.

The therapist reminds the client of her previously stated goal and that this is based on her rational belief.

Client: That's right.

Therapist: So if you want to feel concerned rather than anxious about your boss being cross and otherwise negative with you, what are we going to have to question and change?

The therapist capitalizes on the client's understanding of the iB–emotional problem and rB–emotional goal connections to help the client prepare for disputing.

Client: Belief number 1.

Therapist: Excellent.

Step 15 | Question iB and rB

After conducting a thorough assessment of the specific example of the target problem, identifying and assessing any meta-emotional problems, and teaching the B–C connection, your next step is to begin to question your client's beliefs, both irrational and rational. Because therapeutic time is often at a premium, we suggest that you question your client's premise (i.e., rigid belief) and the one derivative (i.e., awfulizing belief, discomfort-intolerance belief, or depreciation belief) that best accounts for his problem. You will need to negotiate this latter point with your client.

Work to achieve the goals of questioning

The major goal of questioning at this stage of the REBT treatment process is to encourage your client to understand that his irrational belief is unproductive (i.e., it leads to self-defeating emotions), illogical (i.e., it does not make sense), and unrealistic (i.e., it is inconsistent with reality) and that the alternative to this belief (i.e., a rational belief) is productive, logical, and realistic.

If you succeed in helping your client to achieve such an understanding at this stage, do not assume that his conviction in the rational belief will be strong. Help your client to distinguish between light conviction and deep conviction in a rational belief. Also encourage him to see that, at this stage, even a light conviction in an alternative rational belief (i.e., intellectual understanding) is a sign of progress, albeit insufficient in itself to promote emotional and behavioral change.

With specific regard to the target problem, the goals of questioning are to help your client understand the following:

1. Rigid beliefs: Help your client to understand that there is no evidence in support of his absolute demand, whereas evidence does exist for his nondogmatic preferences. (As Ellis used to say: "There are most likely no absolute musts in the universe.") Help your client to see that if his musts were true, then what he was demanding would have to happen—an idea that is patently ridiculous.

2. Awfulizing beliefs: Help your client to understand that what he has defined as awful (i.e., 100 percent bad) is magical nonsense and that, in reality, all experience lies within a 0–99.99 percent range of badness. Another way of addressing this issue is to show the client that "awful" means that his personal world has been shattered beyond repair (which is untrue) and that no good can possibly ever come from the "awful" event (which is also untrue).

3. Discomfort-intolerance beliefs: Help your client to understand that when he holds a discomfort-intolerance belief and thinks he cannot stand something, he believes that he will die, disintegrate, or forfeit his capacity for future happiness. All three possibilities are remote, even when he keeps telling himself, "I can't stand it."

4. Depreciation beliefs: Help your client to understand that when he depreciates himself, others, or life conditions, he is giving himself, others, and life conditions a negative global rating. Not only is such a rating untrue (e.g., "If it were true that I am bad, then this would be my essence, and I could not possibly do good things"), but it is also illogical. In other words, it rates the whole of something on the basis of a part (e.g., "You are bad because you acted badly") and yields poor emotional, behavioral, and cognitive consequences.

Once the irrational belief has been questioned, your client needs to learn to replace it with a new, rational belief. Work together to construct a rational belief that is most adaptive with respect to the adversity at A.* After you have helped your client construct an alternative rational belief, question it logically, empirically, and pragmatically to

---

* Please note that if you used the choice-based assessment technique described in Step 14, you would already have done this.

confirm its rational status. It is much better for your client to see for himself the evidence that rational beliefs are more likely to help his goal-directed behavior than for you to tell him so. Irrational and rational beliefs can also be questioned concurrently instead of consecutively. When you choose the concurrent method, you can ask your client which belief is true and which is false, which is logical and which is illogical, and which is helpful and which is unhelpful. Ensure that you elicit from your client the reasons for each answer.

Rational beliefs in REBT consist of nondogmatic preferences and their derivatives and act as flexible alternatives to rigid musts and their derivatives:

1. Nondogmatic preferences: Help your client to understand that nondogmatic preferences are flexible and suggest what we want to happen (e.g., "I want a new car") and what we do not want to happen (e.g., "I don't want my partner to leave me"). However, in order for your client to grasp the rationality of a preferential statement, it is important for him to state it in its complete form: "I want a new car, but there's no reason why I must have one" and "I don't want my partner to leave me, but there's no reason why she must not leave me." The danger in expressing what we call a partial-preference form is that it can easily be converted to a rigid demand (e.g., "I want a new car [and therefore I must have one]"). The stronger the partial preference, the more likely it is that we will change it into a demand.

2. Nonawfulizing beliefs: Help your client to understand that nonawfulizing refers to evaluating adversities as bad or tragic, but not the end of the world (e.g., "Things are pretty bleak in my life at the moment, but not awful"). Such evaluation is realistic and helps people to change aspects of reality that can be changed or modified. Nonawfulizing also implies that some good can sometimes come from the adversities that happen to us and that, although our lives may have been battered by these bad things, they have not been shattered beyond repair by them.

3. Discomfort-tolerance beliefs: Help your client to understand that discomfort tolerance means learning to increase his ability to withstand discomfort and hardship in life and realizing that he can still enjoy some measure of happiness and stability (e.g., "I certainly don't like the pressure I'm under at the moment, but I can

stand it and learn to deal with it constructively instead of blowing my top"). Acquiring discomfort tolerance helps your client to endure the effort involved in reaching his goals.

4. Acceptance beliefs: Help your client to understand that acceptance refers to seeing himself and others as fallible and in a state of flux. Therefore, it is futile to give himself or others a single global rating, as this rating can never fully describe or encompass the totality of what it means to be human (e.g., "Even though my partner left me, I refuse to condemn myself as worthless because of it. I am too complex to be rated in any way"). He can choose to rate his and others' traits or actions, if this is deemed to be helpful in some way (e.g., "Being impulsive can be very counterproductive at times, so I will learn to take things slower before making a decision"), but it is not realistic, logical, or helpful to rate the whole of a person on the basis of a part of him or her. Also, help your client to see that acceptance of life conditions involves viewing those conditions as being composed of a complex mixture of negative, positive, and neutral events.

Much later in the treatment process (at a point beyond the scope of this primer), your goal will be to help your client internalize a broad range of rational beliefs so that those beliefs become part of a general philosophy of rational living.

Make good use of questions

Let us assume that you are going to question your client's irrational belief in the form of a must. The first stage in the questioning sequence is to ask for evidence in support of the must. Standard questions designed to accomplish this include the following: "Where is the evidence that you must be loved?" "Where is the proof?" "Is it true that you must?" and "Where is it written that you must?"

Ensure that your client answers the question you have asked. For example, in response to the question "Why must you succeed?" she might reply, "Because it would bring me advantages if I succeed." Note that your client has not answered the question you actually asked but has answered a different question, namely, "Why is it preferable for you to succeed?" In fact, it is a good idea to anticipate that your client will not immediately provide a correct answer to your question—a fact borne out by our clinical experience.

According to REBT theory, the only correct answer to the question "Why must you succeed?" is "There is no reason why I must succeed, although I very much want to." If your client gives any other answer, you may need to educate her concerning why her answer is either (a) incorrect with respect to the question you have asked or (b) a correct response to a different question. During this process, use a combination of questions and short didactic explanations until your client gives the correct answer and understands and agrees with this answer. (Understanding why the answer is correct is not the same as agreeing with it.)

As part of this process, again help your client to distinguish between her rational and irrational beliefs. One way of doing this would be to write down (on an easel or chalkboard, for example) the following two questions:

1. Why must you succeed?
2. Why is it preferable, but not essential, for you to succeed?

Ask your client to answer these questions. It is likely that she will give you the same answer to both. If so, help her to see that the reasons she has given constitute evidence for her rational belief, but not for her irrational belief. As we have already stressed, help her to understand that the only answer to a question about the existence of musts is, to quote Ellis, "There are most likely no absolute musts in the universe (one's own or the cosmos)...." Once this understanding has been achieved, help your client to answer questions regarding the rational nature of her flexible beliefs. More precisely, help her to see that there is evidence in favor of both the partial-preference component of her nondogmatic preference (e.g., "It is important that I do well . . .") and the negation of her demand (e.g., ". . . but I don't have to do so").

Be persistent in questioning premise or derivatives

We noted earlier that it is important to question your client's irrational beliefs in the form of both her premise (rigid belief) and at least one of her three derivatives from that premise (awfulizing belief, discomfort-intolerance belief, or depreciation belief). Now, if you have decided to question the irrational premise before beginning to question a derivative from the premise, persist nondogmatically until you have shown your client that there is no evidence in support of her premise. Similarly, if you have chosen to question your client's rational premise first, show her that there is evidence in support of her premise before moving on to question the main derivative from the rational premise.

Switching from premise to derivative (and from derivative to premise) can be confusing for the client. However, if you have persisted in questioning an irrational premise and it becomes clear that your client is not finding this helpful, you may wish to redirect your focus toward a derivative and then monitor your client's reactions. Some clients find it easier to understand why these derivatives are irrational than why their musts are irrational. In the same way, if your client finds it hard to understand why her nondogmatic preference (premise) is rational, then it may be more enlightening for her to concentrate on discussing a derivative (e.g., self-acceptance) from the premise.

Use a variety of questioning strategies

There are three basic questioning strategies. It is best to use all three if you can.

1. Focus on logic: Your purpose here is to help your client to understand why her irrational belief is illogical and her rational belief is logical. Help your client to see that just because she wants something to happen, it does not logically follow that it absolutely must happen. Ask the question "Where is the logic?" rather than "Where is the evidence?" For example, you can show your client that her must about her partial preference is magical in nature, whereas her nondogmatic preference is connected logically to this partial preference, as it avoids the making of a non sequitur.

2. Focus on empiricism: Your goal here is to show your client that her musts and associated derivatives from these musts are almost always empirically inconsistent with reality. As such, use questions that ask your client to provide evidence in support of her irrational beliefs (e.g., "Where is the evidence?"). For instance, help your client understand that if evidence existed to support her belief that she must succeed, then she would have to succeed no matter what she believed. If she is not succeeding at present, then

that fact constitutes evidence that her irrational belief is empirically inconsistent with reality. With regard to your client's non-dogmatic preferences and associated derivatives, show her that these are empirically consistent with reality because, with regard to the example discussed here, she can prove (1) that it is preferable for her to succeed and (2) that she does not have to succeed.

3. Focus on pragmatism: The purpose of focusing on the pragmatic consequences of your client's holding irrational beliefs is to show her that, as long as she believes in her irrational musts and their derivatives, she is going to remain disturbed. Ask questions such as "Where is believing that you must succeed going to get you, other than making you anxious and depressed?" Help your client to see that by endorsing rational beliefs, the probable consequences for her will be reductions in the frequency, intensity, and duration of her emotional disturbance and corresponding increases in her healthy emotional responses.

Use a variety of questioning styles

Although many individual variations are possible, four basic styles of questioning are used to question your client's irrational and rational beliefs.

Socratic style

When you use the Socratic style of questioning, your main task is to ask questions concerning the illogical, empirically inconsistent, and dysfunctional aspects of your client's irrational beliefs and the logical, empirically consistent, and functional aspects of her rational beliefs. The purpose of this style is to encourage your client to think for herself rather than to accept your viewpoint just because you have some authority as a therapist. Although this approach depends mainly on questions, brief explanations designed to correct your client's misconceptions may also be included.

Didactic style

Although REBT therapists prefer the Socratic style, asking questions does not always prove productive. If it does not, you may have to shift to giving more lengthy didactic explanations concerning the reasons that an irrational belief is self-defeating and that a rational belief is more productive. Indeed, you will probably have to use didactic explanations to varying degrees with all of your clients at some point in the treatment process.

When you use didactic explanations, be sure that your client understands what you have been saying by asking him to paraphrase your points. You might say, for example, "I'm not sure whether I'm making myself clear here—perhaps you could put into your own words what you think I've been saying to you." Do not accept without question your client's nonverbal and paraverbal signs of understanding (e.g., head nods, mm-hmms) as evidence that he has in fact understood you. As one of us (R. D.) often says, "There is no good course without a test!" Such "tests" help your client to become an active participant in, rather than a passive recipient of, didactic explanations of aspects of REBT.

Humorous style

With some clients, a productive way of making the point that there is no evidence for irrational beliefs is to use humor or humorous exaggeration. As Walen et al. (1992) note:

> If the client says, "It's really awful that I failed the test!" the therapist might respond, "You're right! It's not only awful, but I don't see how you're going to survive. That's the worst news I've ever heard! This is so horrendous that I can't bear to talk about it. Let's talk about something else, quick!" Such paradoxical statements frequently point out the senselessness of the irrational belief to the client, and very little further debate may be necessary to make the point. (p. 164)

Use humorous exaggeration as a questioning strategy only if (1) you have established a good relationship with your client, (2) your client has already shown some evidence that she has a sense of humor, and (3) your humorous intervention is directed at the irrationality of the client's belief and not at the client as a person.

Self-disclosing style

Another constructive way of questioning your client's irrational beliefs involves therapist self-disclosure. In the coping model of self-disclosure, you reveal that (1) you have experienced a problem similar to your client's, (2) you once held an irrational belief similar to your client's, and (3) you changed your belief and no longer have the problem. For example, one of us (W. D.) has used the personal example of overcoming anxiety about stammering in public (Dryden, 1990):

> I disclose that I used to believe "I must not stammer." I stress that this belief increased rather than diminished my anxiety. I then show how I questioned this irrational belief by proving to myself that there was no evidence to support it, then changed it to the following rational belief: "There is no reason why I must not stammer. If I stammer, I stammer. That's unfortunate, but hardly awful." I then describe how I pushed myself to put this rational belief into practice while speaking in public and finally outline the productive effects that I experienced by doing so.

The coping model of self-disclosure contrasts with a mastery model. In the latter model, you disclose that you have never experienced a problem similar to your client's because you have always thought rationally about the problem at hand. The mastery model tends to accentuate the differences between you and your client and, in our experience, is less productive than the coping model in encouraging your client to challenge her own irrationality. However, some of your clients will not find even the coping model useful. If this is the case, avoid self-disclosure as a questioning strategy and use other strategies instead.

Be creative

The more experience you gain in questioning irrational and rational beliefs, the more you will develop your own individual style of questioning. Thus you will build up a repertoire of stories, aphorisms, metaphors, and other examples to show your clients why their irrational beliefs are self-defeating and why rational alternatives will promote psychological health.

For example, in working with clients who believe they must not experience panic and could not stand it if they did, one of us (W. D.) uses a technique called the Terrorist Dispute:

> I say, "Let's suppose that your parents have been captured by radical terrorists, and these radicals will release your parents only if you agree to put up with 10 panic attacks.

Will you agree to these terms?" The client almost always says yes. If so, I will then say, "But I thought you couldn't stand the experience of panic." The client usually replies: "Well, but I would do it in order to save my parents." To which I respond, "Yes, but will you do it for your own mental health?"

Another creative questioning strategy is what we call the Friend Dispute (Dryden, 2000), an approach that is useful for pointing out to clients the existence of unreasonable self-standards:

Imagine that your client has failed an important test and believes, "I must do well, and I am no good if I don't." Ask her whether she would condemn her best friend for a similar failure in the same way she condemns herself. Normally, your client will say no. If so, point out that she has a different attitude toward her friend than she has toward herself. Suggest that if she chose to be as compassionate toward herself as she is toward her friend, she would be better able to help herself solve her own emotional problems.

We end this section on questioning irrational and rational beliefs with one piece of advice: Before trying to be too creative, master the basics.

| Step 16 | Prepare Your Client to Deepen Conviction in Rational Beliefs |

Once your client has acknowledged that (1) there is no evidence in support of his irrational beliefs but there is evidence to support his rational beliefs, (2) it would be more logical for him to think rationally, and (3) his rational beliefs will lead him to more productive emotional results than will his irrational beliefs, then you are in a position to help him deepen his conviction in his rational beliefs.

Help your client understand why weak conviction will not promote change

Start by helping your client to understand why a weak conviction in rational beliefs, although important, is insufficient to promote change. Do this by discussing briefly the REBT view of therapeutic change. Using Socratic questioning and brief didactic explanations (see Step 15), help your client to see that he will strengthen his conviction in his rational beliefs by questioning his irrational beliefs and replacing them with their rational alternatives within and between therapy sessions. Also, help your client to understand that this process will require him to act against his irrational beliefs, as well as to question them cognitively. Establishing this point now will help you later, when you encourage your client to put his new learning into practice through homework assignments (Step 18) and as you facilitate the working-through process (Step 20).

Deal with the "head–gut" issue

As you help your client to think more rationally, he may say something like "I understand my rational belief will help me to achieve

my goals, but I don't really believe in it yet," or "I believe it intellec-
tually but not emotionally," or "I believe it in my head but don't feel
it in my gut." Indeed, you may wish to bring up this point yourself as
a prelude to discussing with your client how he is going to deepen his
conviction in his rational belief and weaken his conviction in his irrational one. You might ask, for example, "What do you think you will
have to do in order to get your new rational belief into your gut?"

Encourage your client to commit himself to a process of therapeutic change that requires him to question his irrational beliefs
repeatedly and forcefully and to practice thinking rationally in relevant life contexts. As described in Step 18, this process will involve
undertaking a variety of homework assignments.

Step 17 | Check the Validity of A

In Step 8, we emphasized the importance of encouraging your client to assume temporarily that her A is true, even if it is a clear distortion of reality. This is done to identify the irrational belief (B), which largely determines her UNE at C. However, once you have helped your client to question her irrational belief and to identify what she needs to do in order to internalize her new rational belief, you can revisit the A (located in Step 8) and help your client to check its validity by asking some of the following questions:

► How realistic was your A?

► How else could you have viewed this situation?

► How likely is it that your inference is true?

► Would 12 objective observers conclude that your inference was true? If not, what would they have said was a more accurate inference, given all the evidence at hand?

► If you asked someone whom you could trust to give an independent opinion of the truth or falsity of your inference, what might this person say to you?

► If someone told you that she had made the same inference about the same situation that you faced, what would you say to this person about the validity of her inference?

► What information do you need to collect in order to check the validity of your inference, and how reliable will such information be?

If your client still adheres to her inferential distortions about A, which, in REBT terms, stem from her irrational belief, return to examining this belief, because it represents the main target of therapeutic questioning. Once this belief has been attenuated or removed, any lingering inferential distortions can be dealt with. The basic REBT point here is that distorted inferences at A are best dealt with when your client can think more rationally about A.

Step 18

Negotiate a Homework Assignment

Your client is now ready to put his rational belief into practice. Remind him again that the rational emotive behavioral theory of change holds that, in order to deepen his conviction in his rational belief, he needs to practice questioning his irrational belief and strengthening his rational belief in situations that are the same or similar to the A already assessed. Help your client to choose from among a wide variety of homework assignments advocated in REBT:

1. Cognitive assignments: These vary in complexity and structure. One typical cognitive assignment would involve having the client practice his newly learned rational beliefs by attempting to convince someone else of their rationality. Another might involve having the client rehearse rational self-statements before confronting a problematic situation. (See Ellis, 1988, and Ellis & Dryden, 1997, for additional examples.)

2. Imagery assignments: These involve your client's deliberate attempts to change a UNE to an HNE, all the while vividly imagining the adversity at A. These assignments are particularly helpful when you wish to encourage your client to become confident enough so that he can carry out an in vivo assignment. (See Maultsby & Ellis, 1974, and Walen et al., 1992, for further discussion.)

3. Emotive-evocative assignments: These involve the client forcefully and vigorously questioning his irrational beliefs in situations in which he experiences UNE's. (See Ellis & Dryden, 1997.)

4. Behavioral assignments: In these assignments your client, as far as he is prepared to, confronts fully and immediately the

troublesome situations about which he makes himself disturbed, while simultaneously questioning forcefully any irrational beliefs in these contexts. If your client is reluctant or refuses to undertake this type of assignment, you can encourage him to choose an alternate task that he feels is challenging but not overwhelming. However, try to persuade your client to carry out an assignment that involves at least some discomfort. Whatever behavioral assignment you negotiate with your client, ensure that it is both legal and ethical.

Ensure that homework assignments are relevant

Make sure that homework assignments are relevant to the irrational belief targeted for change and that, if the client carries out these assignments, doing so will help him deepen his conviction in the rational alternative (i.e., his rational belief).

Collaborate with your client

While you are discussing appropriate homework assignments with your client, enlist his active collaboration in the process. Ensure that he can see the sense of carrying out the homework assignment and that, if he does so, the experience will help him to achieve his goals; and be sure that he has some degree of confidence that he will be able to execute the agreed-on assignment. Maximize the chances that your client will complete the assignment by helping him to specify when he will do it, in which context, and how frequently.

Be prepared to compromise

An ideal homework assignment will involve the client's actively and forcefully questioning his irrational beliefs in the most relevant contexts possible. Try to encourage your client to carry out an ideal assignment. If this is not possible, urge him to (a) question his irrational beliefs in situations that approximate the most relevant A or (b) use imagery and question his irrational beliefs while vividly imagining A. You may find that if your client does these less-than-ideal assignments, he will be more likely later on to a carry out a more challenging or even ideal assignment.

Assess and troubleshoot obstacles

While you are negotiating appropriate homework assignments with your client, help him to specify any obstacles that might serve as impediments to homework completion. Encourage your client to find possible ways of overcoming these obstacles in advance of carrying out each assignment.

Use homework at different times during therapy

For the purpose of discussion, we have focused on homework assignments that involve your client's strengthening his conviction in his rational beliefs. However, you can employ such assignments at any point during the treatment sequence. Specifically, you might encourage your client to execute homework assignments to help him (1) pinpoint his troublesome emotions at C, (2) detect his irrational beliefs at B, and (3) identify the most relevant aspect of the situation (i.e., A) about which he has made himself disturbed.

You may also employ homework assignments as part of a process in which you educate your client about the ABC's of REBT. In this case, you could ask your client to read various books (bibliotherapy) or listen to REBT lectures on CDs or MP3 files. When doing so, choose material that is relevant to your client's problem and that he can readily understand. If no appropriate material is available, you might even create written materials or audio materials to address your client's particular problem.

Step 19 | Check Homework Assignments

Once you have negotiated a particular homework assignment with your client and she has undertaken it, use the beginning of the next session to check what she has learned from the experience. If you fail to do this, you show your client that you do not consider homework assignments to be an important ingredient in the process of change, when, in fact, they are central to it.

Verify that your client faced A

As noted earlier, clients are prone to develop strategies to avoid adversities at A rather than strategies to confront the A and change C. Homework assignments, at this stage, are primarily designed to solve emotional problems, not practical problems. Therefore, when you check on your client's experience in carrying out an assignment, make sure she actually faced, as far as was possible, the adversity at A that she committed herself to confront. If your client has done this, she will usually report that she first made herself disturbed and then made herself undisturbed in the same situation by using the questioning techniques discussed in therapy. If your client has not done so, point this out to her, deal with any obstacles involved, and encourage her to confront the situation once more and use vigorous questioning to make herself undisturbed in that context. If necessary, model appropriate questions and encourage your client to rehearse these in the session and before facing the situation in question.

Verify that your client changed B

If your client reports a successful experience in carrying out the home-work assignment, assess whether her success can be attributed to her (a) changing her irrational belief to its rational alternative, (b) chang-ing either the situation or her inferences at A about the situation, or (c) using distraction techniques. If your client used the latter two methods, acknowledge her efforts but point out that these methods may not be helpful in the long term. Stress that practical solutions or distractions are only palliative, because if an individual has not learned to change the UNE associated with the situation, the solution is not a permanent one. If unpleasant or aversive A's are unavoidable, the emo-tional problem will only reassert itself. Once again, encourage the client to face the situation in which her A is embedded, but this time elicit her commitment that she will question her irrational belief and practice acting on the basis of the new rational belief.

Deal with failure to complete homework assignments

If your client has failed to execute the agreed-on homework assignment, accept her as a fallible human being and help her to identify the rea-sons she did not carry out the assignment. Use the Situational ABC framework to encourage your client to focus on possible irrational beliefs that served to prevent her from carrying out the assignment. Assess, in particular, whether your client held irrational beliefs indi-cating a philosophy of discomfort intolerance (e.g., "It was too hard"; "I couldn't be bothered"; "I absolutely shouldn't have to put this much energy into therapy"). If your client holds such beliefs, encourage her to challenge and change them, then reassign the homework.

| Step 20 | Facilitate the Working-through Process |

For your client to achieve enduring therapeutic change, he needs to challenge and change his irrational beliefs repeatedly and forcefully in relevant contexts in which the adversity occurs at A. In doing so, he will further strengthen his conviction in rational beliefs and continue to weaken his conviction in irrational ones. The purpose of this working-through process is for your client to integrate rational beliefs into his emotional and behavioral repertoire.

Suggest different homework assignments for the same irrational belief

When your client has achieved some success at questioning his irrational belief in relevant situations in which the adversity at A occurs, suggest that he use different homework assignments to encourage change in the same belief. Doing so serves to teach your client that he can use a variety of methods to question the target irrational belief, as well as other irrational beliefs that may emerge during the course of therapy. In addition, such variety may help to sustain his interest in the change process.

Discuss the nonlinear model of change

It is important that your client has a realistic view of the change process, one that will encourage him to keep going when the going gets tough in therapy. Thus we suggest that you explain that change is nonlinear and that your client will probably experience some difficulties in sustaining his success at questioning his irrational beliefs in a wide range of contexts. Identify possible setbacks and help your client develop ways of handling these setbacks. In particular, help your client to pinpoint and challenge the irrational beliefs that might underpin these relapses (e.g., "I absolutely shouldn't have to keep working this hard to change!").

In addition, explain that change can be evaluated on three major dimensions:

1. Frequency: Does your client make himself disturbed less frequently than he did before?
2. Intensity: When your client makes himself disturbed, does he do so with less intensity than before?
3. Duration: When your client makes himself disturbed, does he do so for shorter periods of time than before?

Using these three criteria of change, encourage your client to keep records of his disturbed emotions at C in the Situational ABC framework. At this point, it is also helpful to have your client read *How to Maintain and Enhance Your Rational-Emotive Therapy Gains* (Ellis, 1984b). This booklet includes many useful suggestions to help your client facilitate his own working-through process.

Encourage your client to take responsibility for continued progress

At this stage, you can help your client to develop his own homework assignments to change his target belief and to change other irrational beliefs in different situations. Thus, if your client has been successful at questioning an irrational belief about approval in a work-related situation in which he faces criticism, you could encourage him to question this belief in other situations in which he may encounter criticism (e.g., with strangers or friends). The more your client develops and executes his own homework assignments, the more he will begin to serve as his own therapist. This accomplishment is important because, as an REBT therapist, your long-term goal is to encourage your client to internalize the REBT model of change and to take responsibility for further progress after therapy has ended.

Part III

CASE EXAMPLE

In the final part of this primer, we present actual case material to illustrate the rational emotive behavioral treatment sequence described in Part II. Although a single case cannot illustrate all the points discussed, we believe that the case chosen does cover the most salient issues. In order to demonstrate clearly the steps in the REBT treatment sequence, we deliberately selected a case in which the client responded well to REBT.

The client, Karen (a pseudonym), was referred to me (W. D.) by her general practitioner, whom she had consulted for problems of sleeplessness and general tension. At the time of the referral, Karen was 26 years old and worked as a laboratory technician at a local college. She lived at home with her parents, did not have a partner, but did have several close friends of the same sex whom she had recently been avoiding. Karen had never sought therapy before.

Before beginning the treatment process, I greeted Karen and discovered how she came to be referred to me. Then we discussed her expectations for therapy and agreed on a fee appropriate to her situation.

STEP 1: ASK FOR A PROBLEM

After dealing with these initial practicalities, I then asked Karen what problem she would like to start with. She said that she had been having trouble sleeping during the past few months and had been avoiding social contact with other people, including her close friends. She traced the development of these problems back to the end of her relationship with Pete, her fiancé, who had left her for another woman 3 months earlier.

STEP 2: CLARIFY AND SELECT THE TARGET PROBLEM

I commented that Karen had several problems and suggested that we list them so that we could deal with them one by one. Karen thought this was a good idea, and we developed the following problem list:

1. Feelings of hurt about the breakup of my relationship with Pete
2. Avoiding contact with my friends
3. Sleeplessness
4. General tension

I again asked Karen which problem she would like to start with, and she chose the problem of avoiding contact with her friends. This issue thus became the initial target problem of therapy.

STEP 3: FORMULATE THE TARGET PROBLEM

I asked Karen to tell me a little more about the problem, and the following dialogue ensued:

Karen: Well, ever since Pete dumped me, I've just not felt like seeing anyone, least of all my friends. Part of me wants to see them because I miss them very much, but another part of me just wants to hibernate.

W. D.:   But let's suppose that you did go to see your friends. What feelings do you think you might experience?

Karen: I'm not sure. I think I would be very uncomfortable.

W. D.:   And then what would happen?

Karen: I'd just make some excuse to go home again.

W. D.:   So it may be that what you call avoidance of social contact with your friends really has to do with your avoiding uncomfortable feelings that you think you would experience.

Karen: That seems right.

Putting this into the Situational ABC framework for formulating problems, we have:

Situation: The prospect of seeing friends

A: Predicting that I will have uncomfortable feelings

B: Yet to be discovered

C: Avoidance

STEP 4: SET A GOAL WITH RESPECT TO THE FORMULATED PROBLEM

Client goal selection at this stage is usually provisional, because information related to the target problem is often insufficient to gain a clear picture of the determinants of the problem.

W. D.:   So what would you like to do about these uncomfortable feelings that you think you will experience?

Karen: Well, it would be helpful to deal with them and not run away from them so that I can choose whether or not to see my friends from a healthier outlook.

W. D.:   That seems like a good idea.

Putting this into the Situational ABC framework for formulating goals, we have:

Situation: The prospect of seeing friends

A: Predicting that I will have uncomfortable feelings

B: Yet to be discovered

C: Stay and deal with these feelings rather than avoid them

STEP 5: ASK FOR A SPECIFIC EXAMPLE OF THE TARGET PROBLEM

Up to this point, Karen had spoken about the uncomfortable feelings she would experience if she visited her friends. The next step was to anchor the target problem in a specific example in order to move counseling from the general to the concrete.

> W. D.:   Can you think of a specific occasion when you experienced these uncomfortable feelings that resulted in avoidance?
>
> Karen: About a week ago I was invited by some friends to go to a party.
>
> W. D.:   Did you accept?
>
> Karen: No. I felt safer at home, hibernating.
>
> W. D.:   That seems a good example to focus on.

STEP 6: ASSESS THE SITUATION

The party was going to be in the home of Susan, one of Karen's friends, and, as far as Karen could tell, about 20 people would be there, including Karen's other female friends.

STEP 7: ASSESS C

My hypothesis at this point was that Karen's social avoidance served to help her to avoid negative feelings. I next moved on to obtain a more precise assessment of these feelings.

> W. D.:   Now, if you were to go to the party and meet with your close friends and remain with them, and you really let yourself experience those uncomfortable feelings that you mentioned, what kind of feelings would they be?
>
> Karen: I'm not sure.
>
> W. D.:   Well, close your eyes and see yourself with your friends; really try to picture yourself and picture them. Try to imagine that you are with them right now. What are you experiencing?
>
> Karen: (Pauses.) It's funny—I feel anxious.

STEP 8: ASSESS A

As shown in the previous step, Karen had been able to identify the feeling of anxiety as the C in the situation. My next step was to help her to identify what she felt most anxious about at A.

> W. D.: Now open your eyes. You seem surprised to learn that you would feel anxious. What do you think you would be anxious about?
>
> Karen: Well, when you asked me to picture my friends, I had an image of them talking about my fiancé going off with another woman.
>
> W. D.: Well, what one thing would you need to reduce or eliminate your anxiety in this situation?
>
> Karen: Well, if they did not look down on me.
>
> W. D.: So, are you most anxious about them looking down on you because your fiancé went off with another woman?
>
> Karen: Exactly.
>
> W. D.: Right, and as we look at it now with them looking down at you, what feelings go along with that?
>
> Karen: (Pauses.) Shame. Yes, I'd feel very ashamed.

Note that Karen's C has changed from anxiety to shame. This frequently happens when the client's disturbed feeling involves anxiety. As shown in Appendix 1, anxiety occurs when the person has an irrational belief about some future threat. When, in the context of exploring the client's A, the therapist asks the client to assume that the threat has occurred, the client's feeling changes to reflect this assumption. For example, Karen would be anxious about the prospect that her friends would look down on her but would feel ashamed if that event had actually taken place.

STEP 9: AGREE UPON A GOAL WITH RESPECT TO THE ASSESSED PROBLEM

In Step 4, it was agreed that the goal ("I want to deal with my uncomfortable feelings and not avoid them so that I can decide whether or not to see my friends from a healthier outlook") was based on the formulated problem. In the current step, goal selection was based on the information revealed about the nature of Karen's anxiety (C) during the assessment of A. I decided to treat Karen's C as shame and thus encouraged her to assume that A (her friends' looking down on her) had actually occurred. My next task was to encourage her to feel disappointed, rather than ashamed, about this situation should it occur (new goal).

W. D.: Now, as long as you feel ashamed in the face of your friends looking down on you, it makes sense for you to avoid them. Can you see that?

Karen: Yes.

W. D.: But let's see what alternatives you have about handling the situation in which they look down on you. I want to stress, however, that we're assuming for the moment that they *would* look down on you. Realistically, they may very well not, but let's assume that they would. What productive feelings could you strive to experience instead of shame?

Karen: To be indifferent toward them?

W. D.: But is that realistic? Do you think you could ever be indifferent about what your close friends think of you?

Karen: No, I guess not.

W. D.: What else could you feel instead of shame?

Karen: I'm not sure.

W. D.: How about feeling disappointed? My guess is that, if you felt disappointed, but not ashamed, in the face of them looking down on you, you wouldn't run away, and you would be in a position to try to persuade them that they were wrong to disapprove of you, something you couldn't do if you were ashamed.

Karen: Yes, that makes sense, but how do I get myself to feel disappointed rather than ashamed?

STEP 10: HELP YOUR CLIENT TO SEE THE LINK BETWEEN THE FORMULATED PROBLEM GOAL AND THE ASSESSED PROBLEM GOAL

Because there had been two goal-setting stages (Steps 4 and 9), Karen seemed confused about how two different goals for change had emerged. I attempted to show Karen how they were linked.

W. D.: The first goal, of dealing with your uncomfortable feelings before deciding whether or not to see your friends from an undisturbed viewpoint, was agreed on after just skimming the surface of your problem. When the problem was explored in depth through the use of a specific example, we discovered that you would feel ashamed if your friends looked down on you.

Karen: Okay, so far so good.

W. D.: So if you feel disappointed instead of ashamed about your friends looking down on you, you will not be emotionally disturbed about the situation, and therefore you would be dealing better with your uncomfortable feelings, which, in turn, will help you decide whether you want to see your friends or not. That's how the two goals are linked.

Karen: So if I try to feel disappointed about the situation instead of ashamed, then I can see things more clearly and make better decisions for myself.

W. D.: Exactly.

STEP 11: IDENTIFY AND ASSESS ANY META-EMOTIONAL PROBLEMS IF RELEVANT

From her question at the end of Step 9, it seemed that Karen was ready to move toward considering how she could change her feelings of shame to those of disappointment. Thus I did not at this point assess the presence of a meta-emotional problem. I did so later on and found that Karen did not have a meta-emotional problem about her shame or social avoidance.

STEP 12: TEACH THE B–C CONNECTION

In the process of teaching the B–C connection, I used an example unrelated to Karen's own problem. By doing so, I hoped to help her understand with greater objectivity the distinction between rational and irrational beliefs.

W. D.: The first step to changing your feelings from shame to disappointment is to understand what determines your feelings. Now, would a hundred women of your age all feel ashamed if their friends looked down on them, assuming that for all of them, their friends' opinions were important?

Karen: No, I guess not.

W. D.: Why not?

Karen: Well, people react to the same situation in different ways.

W. D.: Right, but what determines these different reactions?

Karen: I don't know.

W. D.: Well, psychologists have done a lot of research that tends to confirm what the ancient philosopher Epictetus said—that people are disturbed not by things but by their views of things. So your views or beliefs about your friends looking down on you determine how you feel. Does that make sense?

Karen: Yes, it does.

W. D.: So, if you want to change your feelings from shame to disappointment, what do you need to consider?

Karen: My beliefs about my friends looking down on me.

W. D.: Right, to change your feelings, you need to change your beliefs. I want first to help you to distinguish between two types of beliefs. One will lead to shame and other self-defeating emotions, whereas the other will lead to disappointment and other constructive emotions. Now, in order to do this, I want to digress for a moment and take you through an example in which I will distinguish between these two types of beliefs. Is that okay?

Karen: Fine.

W. D.: Now, I want you to imagine that you have 10 dollars in your purse and that your belief is that you prefer to have a minimum of 11 dollars at all times, but that it's not absolutely necessary for you to have 11 dollars. How will you feel about having 10 dollars when you want to have 11 dollars?

Karen: Somewhat concerned.

W. D.: But you wouldn't want to kill yourself, right?

Karen: Right.

W. D.:   Now, this time imagine that you believe you absolutely must have a minimum of 11 dollars at all times—you must, you must, you must—and you look in your purse and find that you only have 10 dollars. Now how will you feel?

Karen: Depressed.

W. D.:   Or anxious. Remember that it's the same situation but a different belief. Now imagine that you still have that same absolute belief that you must have a minimum of 11 dollars at all times, and this time you find that you have 12 dollars in your purse. Now how will you feel?

Karen: Relieved.

W. D.:   Right, or pleased. But by holding that same belief that you absolutely must have a minimum of 11 dollars at all times, you think something that leads you to become anxious again. What do you think that thought would be?

Karen: That I might lose 2 dollars?

W. D.:   Right, or you might spend 2 dollars or get robbed. Now the point of this example is that all humans, male or female, rich or poor, black or white, now and in the future, will make themselves emotionally disturbed when they don't get what they believe they must get. And they will also make themselves miserable when they do get it because of their musts—because even when they have what they think they must have, they could always lose it. But when humans have nondogmatic desires and don't transform these desires into dogmatic musts, they will modify what can be changed, adjust constructively to situations that can't be changed, or try to prevent something unpleasant from happening in the future.

STEP 13: ASSESS iB

Once I felt sure through feedback that Karen could distinguish between rational and irrational beliefs, I encouraged her to extrapolate to her own situation.

> W. D.: Now keep in mind this distinction between nondogmatic desires and dogmatic musts as we apply it to your own situation, okay?
>
> Karen: Fine.
>
> W. D.: Now, what do you think the must is about your friends looking down on you that leads to your shame?
>
> Karen: They must not look down on me?
>
> W. D.: Right, and if you believe that, what kind of person do you think you would be in your own mind if they did look down on you?
>
> Karen: No good.

STEP 14: CONNECT iB AND THE EMOTIONAL PROBLEM AND rB AND THE EMOTIONAL GOAL

After teaching the B–C connection and encouraging Karen to apply it to her own situation, I next attempted to solidify the relationship between Karen's irrational beliefs and her feelings of shame at C and the relationship between her alternative rational beliefs and her emotional goal of feeling disappointment rather than shame. Having helped her to understand these connections, I then helped her to see that in order to achieve her emotional goal she would need to change her irrational belief.

> W. D.: So, can you see that as long as you demand that your friends must not look down on you and as long as you believe that you are no good if they do, then you will be ashamed and tend to avoid social contact with them?
>
> Karen: Yes, I can see that.
>
> W. D.: And how would you feel if you believed that you would prefer it if they did not look down on you, but that this does not have to happen?
>
> Karen: I guess I would feel disappointed.
>
> W. D.: And not necessarily avoid social contact with them.
>
> Karen: That's right.
>
> W. D.: So, if you wish to change your feelings of shame to those of disappointment, what do you need to change first?
>
> Karen: My beliefs.

W. D.:   And, more specifically, your beliefs that your friends must not look down on you and that you would be no good if they did.

STEP 15: QUESTION iB AND rB

The next step involved the use of the Socratic and didactic styles of questioning Karen's beliefs.

W. D.:   Right. Now let's take these beliefs one at a time, although they're really linked. I'm going to help you reconsider these beliefs. Let's take the first one, that your friends must not look down on you. There are basically three ways of challenging this belief. The first is to ask whether or not it is logical. Now, don't forget, you have a desire, which is that you don't want your friends to look down on you, right?

Karen: Right.

W. D.:   But does it follow logically that because you don't want your friends to look down on you that they must not do so?

Karen: No, I guess not.

W. D.:   Why not?

Karen: Well, because wanting something not to happen doesn't mean it mustn't happen.

W. D.:   That's it. To demand that something mustn't happen just because we don't want it to happen is to believe in magic.

Karen: Which doesn't exist.

W. D.:   Right. Now let's consider the second way of challenging this belief, which is to ask whether or not it is consistent with reality. Now, if there really were a law of the universe that decreed that your friends absolutely would not look down on you, what could never happen?

Karen: They could never look down on me. Oh, I see . . . I'm demanding that something must not happen which could of course happen.

W. D.:   Right, that's a good insight. You would of course prefer it not to happen, but that doesn't mean that it must not happen, because it always could. Now let's consider the third way of challenging this belief, which is to consider its usefulness. Now, as long as you believe that your friends must not look down on you, what consequences of holding this belief are likely?

Karen: Well, from what we discussed earlier, I'm going to be anxious about it happening and ashamed if it does happen.

W. D.:   And don't forget that it will also lead you to avoid social contact with your friends.

Karen: As has been happening.

W. D.:   Right. So the belief is going to get you into trouble. Now, to sum up: The three ways of challenging or questioning a must involve asking, "Is it logical?" "Is it consistent with reality?" and "Will it give me good results?" Now we've seen that the answer to these three questions is no. But don't take my word for it—consider it for yourself. It is also important to apply these three questions to your nondogmatic preferences. First is your belief "I don't want my friends to look down on me, but there's no reason why they must not do so." Logical?

Karen: Well, it's logical, as long as I have such a desire. It is certainly not magical like my demand was.

W. D.:   Right. Now, is it consistent with reality?

Karen: Well, it is reality that I have such a desire, so my desire exists; so, yes, it is consistent with reality.

W. D.:   Right, and don't forget that such a belief allows for the possibility that your friends may look down on you, which your dogmatic must did not allow for. Finally, what are the likely emotional and behavioral consequences of your belief "I don't want my friends to look down on me, but there's no reason why they must not do so"?

Karen: Well, as we said earlier, it would help me to feel disappointed and would encourage me to try to get my friends to change their minds about me because I would not be avoiding them.

W. D.:   Right. Now let's use our three questions with your second self-defeating belief: "I'm no good if my friends look down on me." First, is it logical to conclude that your whole self is no good just because your friends think badly of you?

Karen: I'm not sure I understand.

W. D.:   Well, let's assume that several of my colleagues are listening to our session today. Let's also assume that they not only think badly of my therapy skills but look down on me as a person. Do I have to agree with them and define myself as "no good"?

Karen: Oh, I see what you mean. I'm agreeing with my friends' definition of me.

W. D.:   Right. Now, if your friends really do look down on you—and remember, we're assuming that they really do—they would have to take a part of you and consider that bad. Then they would jump to the conclusion that because you had this bad part, all of you was bad. Is that good logic on their part?

Karen: No, it's not, because a part can never define the whole.

W. D.:   Right, and don't forget that you then agree with their bad logic.

Karen: Exactly.

W. D.:   You said just now that a part can never define the whole. That's a very good reason not to rate yourself at all, because your self is too complex to be given a single rating.

Karen: So it's okay to rate parts of yourself but not the whole?

W. D.:   Right.

Karen: So, when I say, "I'm no good," I'm rating my whole self?

W. D.:   Right, and the alternative is to accept yourself as an unratable, fallible human being with good and bad aspects. So, if your friends really do look down on you, how can you respond in your own mind?

Karen: Let's see . . . I can accept myself as an unratable, fallible human being, even if others disapprove of me.

W. D.: Right, your self-acceptance belief means that you do not define yourself on the basis of your friends' disapproval. Your definition of yourself is the same whether they approve or disapprove of you.

Karen: Oh, I like that idea. It's very logical.

W. D.: Right. Now let's move on to the second question: If the belief "I'm no good" were consistent with reality, what would you only be able to do in life?

Karen: No good things, and that's obviously not true.

W. D.: Right. So what's the alternative?

Karen: Again, that I'm an unratable, fallible human being who is receiving disapproval, which is bad.

W. D.: But you're not bad just because it is. Now the third question: As long as you believe that you are no good when your friends look down on you, where will that belief get you?

Karen: Anxious and ashamed.

W. D.: And, again, avoiding social contact. But let's also use the three questions with the rational alternative beliefs. Is it logical to conclude that if your friends disapprove of you, you are still an unratable, fallible human being?

Karen: Yes, it is. Their view of me doesn't change me unless I let it. I can see that now.

W. D.: Good. Now, is the belief that you are an unratable, fallible human being in the face of their disapproval consistent with reality?

Karen: Yes, it is. As I said before, I'm still the same, with or without their approval, although their approval would be nice. I am too complex to be defined by their disapproval.

W. D.:   Right. Now, finally, the third point: If you believe that you are fallible and unratable in the face of your friends' disapproval, what emotional and behavioral consequences will result?

Karen: Again, I'd be disappointed but not ashamed, and I'd try to reason with them rather than avoid them.

STEP 16: PREPARE YOUR CLIENT TO DEEPEN CONVICTION IN RATIONAL BELIEFS

In order to help Karen achieve more than an intellectual understanding of her problem, it was necessary to make the point that changing beliefs is a difficult process requiring much practice.

W. D.:   Now, how often do you consider you will have to challenge your self-defeating beliefs before you begin to believe in their rational alternatives?

Karen: Quite often.

W. D.:   Right, and do you know why?

Karen: Because that's what you have to do to change a habit.

W. D.:   Right. Imagine that when you were young, you wanted to learn to play tennis, and your next-door neighbor said that she would teach you. Unfortunately, she taught you all wrong, and, as you were eager, you continually practiced the incorrect strokes, not knowing of course that they were wrong. Years later, you found that your game was getting worse rather than better, so you decided to go to a tennis pro. She was able to diagnose the problem and showed you how to perform the strokes correctly. Now, what would you have to do to improve your tennis?

Karen: Practice the new strokes.

W. D.:   Right, but would you be comfortable performing the new strokes at first?

Karen: I guess not.

W. D.:   Why not?

Karen: Because I'd be used to performing the strokes incorrectly.

W. D.: Right, the old strokes would feel natural. But would that natural feeling stop you from correcting a stroke when you realized that it was incorrect?

Karen: No.

W. D.: Right, and it's the same thing with changing your beliefs. The next time you think about seeing your friends and feel like avoiding them, look for your belief "My friends must not look down on me, and I'd be no good if they did." Realize that this belief has become quite natural to you, but that if you don't go along with that natural feeling, you can identify, challenge, and change that belief. You can keep doing so until the new belief—"I don't want my friends to look down on me, but if they do, I can still accept myself as an unratable, fallible human being"—becomes more natural to you. Also, the more you act according to this new belief, the more you will gain conviction in the belief.

Karen: So I not only need to challenge the old belief in my head, I need to act on the new belief as well.

W. D.: Exactly—until you move from believing the rational belief in your head to really feeling it in your gut and until you can act spontaneously on it.

STEP 17: CHECK THE VALIDITY OF A

After the initial questioning of Karen's irrational and rational beliefs, I suggested we return to check the validity of her A (assessed in Step 8).

W. D.: Do you remember what you were most anxious about when you imagined mixing with your friends instead of avoiding them?

Karen: Yes, that they would look down on me and I would then feel ashamed.

W. D.: Do you think they would actually look down on you?

Karen: Well, one or two might, but most of them wouldn't do that. I can see that now.

W. D.:   Even if your inference about your friends looking down on you is largely false, it is still very important for you to continue working to challenge and change your irrational belief. Do you know why?

Karen: Because I need to learn to accept myself no matter what others—friends or anybody else—may or may not think about me.

W. D.:   Exactly.

STEP 18: NEGOTIATE A HOMEWORK ASSIGNMENT

Karen's ability to challenge her irrational beliefs, along with her understanding that it would be necessary to practice her alternative rational beliefs, showed that she was ready to undertake specific homework assignments.

W. D.:   Now, since changing beliefs takes a lot of work, it's important for you to put into practice between sessions what you learn in sessions. Can you see the sense of that?

Karen: That's what I expected.

W. D.:   Good. Now, does it make sense to apply the three questions "Is it logical?" "Is it consistent with reality?" and "What results will it bring me?" to your self-defeating belief: "My friends must not look down on me, and I'm no good if they do"? And then to apply these three questions to your more constructive alternative belief: "I don't want my friends to look down on me, but there's no reason why they must not. If they do, I can still accept myself as an unratable, fallible human being"?

Karen: Yes, I'd like to review those points.

W. D.:   How often would you like to do it?

Karen: How about three times a day?

W. D.:   When and where will you do it?

Karen: Just before breakfast, lunch, and dinner, wherever I happen to be eating.

W. D.:   Fine. Now, can you see any obstacles to doing this?

Karen: No. I'm sure I can do that.

W. D.: Good. Here is a written list of the questions to use on these occasions.

STEP 19: CHECK HOMEWORK ASSIGNMENTS

At the beginning of the next session, Karen revealed that she had been able to review the three questions as agreed on and that she found the results helpful.

W. D.: How did you get on with the homework assignment?

Karen: Very well. I used the three questions and can see more clearly now why the musts are self-defeating and the nondogmatic preferences more healthy. Also, the self-acceptance idea makes a lot of sense to me, and I've been using this idea with some of my other problems.

STEP 20: FACILITATE THE WORKING-THROUGH PROCESS

Karen was soon ready to use behavioral assignments to overcome her feelings of shame about "her friends looking down on her for being dumped." She very quickly sought out her friends and told them about the breakup of her relationship with her fiancé, having practiced rational emotive imagery first. Here she vividly imagined her friends looking down on her and began to feel ashamed, then changed this feeling to disappointment while still keeping in mind her friends' negative view of her. The imagery helped her to practice changing her irrational belief to its more rational alternative. When she actually told her friends about the breakup, she was delighted to discover that they were in fact very supportive.

Karen also worked through her shame in other situations, such as work. She had previously been reluctant to ask for help whenever she could not solve a work problem. However, as she became able to dispel her shame-creating idea "My supervisor must not think badly of me, and I'd be inferior if he does," she became more willing to disclose her ignorance and ask for help. Once again, Karen was glad to learn that her supervisor was actually pleased with her new attitude of "openness," as he called it.

Karen did not have a problem with low frustration tolerance and thus reported little difficulty in carrying out her homework assignments. Most of your clients will have more difficulty than Karen in putting into practice what they learn in therapy. We suggest that you consult Ellis (2002) for a lengthy discussion of how to overcome client (and therapist) resistance.

EPILOGUE

We have now come to the end of our discussion. If you wish to develop your skills as a rational emotive behavior therapist, then use REBT with your clients, obtain expert supervision of your work, attend advanced REBT training practica, and consult frequently the more advanced texts mentioned throughout this primer. We hope that you have found this basic introduction to REBT instructive and wish you well in your future career as a rational emotive behavior therapist. Good luck!

Appendix 1 | # UNDERSTANDING COMMON EMOTIONAL PROBLEMS AND THEIR HEALTHY ALTERNATIVES

Adversity	Belief	Emotion	Behavior	Subsequent Thinking
Threat to personal domain	Irrational	Anxiety	• You withdraw physically from the threat • You withdraw mentally from the threat • You ward off the threat (e.g., by superstitious behavior) • You tranquilize your feelings • You seek reassurance	• You overestimate the probability of the threat occurring • You underestimate your ability to cope with the threat • You create an even more negative threat in your mind • You have more task-irrelevant thoughts than shown in the rational belief of concern
Threat to personal domain	Rational	Concern	• You face up to the threat • You deal with the threat constructively • You take constructive action to reduce/minimize the risk or danger	• You are realistic about the probability of the threat occurring • You view the threat realistically • You realistically appraise your ability to cope with the threat • You do not create an even more negative threat in your mind • You have more task-relevant thoughts than shown in the irrational belief of anxiety

Adversity	Belief	Emotion	Behavior	Subsequent Thinking
• Loss (with implications for future) • Failure	Irrational	Depression	• You withdraw from reinforcements • You withdraw into yourself • You create an environment consistent with your depressed feelings • You attempt to terminate feelings of depression in self-destructive ways	• You see only negative aspects of the loss or failure • You think of other losses and failures that you have experienced • You think you are unable to help yourself (helplessness) • You see only pain and blackness in the future (hopelessness)
• Loss (with implications for future) • Failure	Rational	Sadness	• You seek out reinforcements after a period of mourning • You express your feelings about the loss or failure and talk about these to significant others	• You are able to recognize both negative and positive aspects of the loss or failure • You think you are able to help youself • You look to the future with hope

Adversity	Belief	Emotion	Behavior	Subsequent Thinking
• Frustration • Goal obstruction • Self or other transgresses personal rule • Threat to self-esteem	Irrational	Problematic anger	• You attack the other(s) physically • You attack the other(s) verbally • You attack the other(s) passive-aggressively • You displace the attack onto another person, animal, or object • You withdraw aggressively • You recruit allies against the other(s)	• You overestimate the extent to which the other(s) acted deliberately • You see malicious intent in the motives of the other(s) • You see yourself as definitely right and the other(s) as definitely wrong • You are unable to see the point of view of the other(s) • You plot to exact revenge
• Frustration • Goal obstruction • Self or other transgresses personal rule • Threat to self-esteem	Rational	Nonproblematic anger	• You assert yourself with the other(s) • You request, but do not demand, behavioral change from the other(s) • You leave an unsatisfactory situation nonaggressively after taking steps to deal with it	• You do not overestimate the extent to which the other(s) acted deliberately • You are able to see the point of view of the other(s) • You do not plot to exact revenge • You do not see malicious intent in the motives of the other(s) • You do not see yourself as definitely right and the other(s) as definitely wrong

Adversity	Belief	Emotion	Behavior	Subsequent Thinking
• Violation of moral code (sin of commission) • Failure to live up to moral code (sin of omission) • Hurts the feelings of a significant other	Irrational	Guilt	• You escape from the unhealthy pain of guilt in self-defeating ways • You beg forgiveness from the person you wronged • You promise unrealistically that you will not "sin" again • You punish yourself physically or by deprivation • You defensively disclaim responsibility for wrongdoing • You reject offers of forgiveness	• You assume that you have definitely committed the sin • You assume more personal responsibility than the situation warrants • You assign far less responsibility to others than is warranted • You do not think of mitigating factors • You do not put your behavior into an overall context • You think that you will receive retribution
• Violation of moral code (sin of commission) • Failure to live up to moral code (sin of omission) • Hurts the feelings of a significant other	Rational	Remorse	• You face up to the healthy pain that accompanies the realization that you have sinned • You ask, but do not beg, for forgiveness • You understand the reasons for wrongdoing and act on your understanding • You atone for the sin by taking a penalty • You make appropriate amends • You do not make excuses for your behavior or enact other defensive behavior • You do accept offers of forgiveness	• You take into account all relevant data when judging whether or not you have "sinned" • You assume an appropriate level of personal responsibility • You assign an appropriate level of responsibility to others • You take into account mitigating factors • You put your behavior into overall context • You do not think you will receive retribution

Adversity	Belief	Emotion	Behavior	Subsequent Thinking
• Something shameful has been revealed about you (or a group with whom you identify) by yourself or by others • Acting in a way that falls very short of your ideal • Others will look down on or shun you (or a group with whom you identify)	Irrational	Shame	• You remove yourself from the "gaze" of others • You isolate yourself from others • You save face by attacking other(s) who have "shamed" you • You defend your threatened self-esteem in self-defeating ways • You ignore attempts by others to restore social equilibrium	• You overestimate the "shamefulness" of the information revealed • You overestimate the likelihood that the judging group will notice or be interested in the information • You overestimate the degree of disapproval you (or your reference group) will receive • You overestimate the length of time any disapproval will last
• Something shameful has been revealed about you (or a group with whom you identify) by yourself or by others • Acting in a way that falls very short of your ideal • Others will look down on or shun you (or a group with whom you identify)	Rational	Disappoint-ment	• You continue to participate actively in social interaction • You respond to attempts of others to restore social equilibrium	• You see the information revealed in a compassionate, self-accepting context • You are realistic about the likelihood that the judging group will notice or be interested in the information revealed • You are realistic about the degree of disapproval you (or reference group) will receive • You are realistic about the length of time any disapproval will last

113

Adversity	Belief	Emotion	Behavior	Subsequent Thinking
Others treat you badly (and you think you do not deserve such treatment)	Irrational	Hurt	• You shut down communication channel with the other • You sulk and make obvious you feel hurt without disclosing details of the matter • You indirectly criticize or punish the other for the offense	• You overestimate the unfairness of the other person's behavior • You think that the other person does not care for you or is indifferent to you • You see yourself as alone, uncared for, or misunderstood • You tend to think of past "hurts" • You expect the other to make the first move toward repairing the relationship
Others treat you badly (and you think you do not deserve such treatment)	Rational	Sorrow	• You communicate your feelings to the other directly • You influence the other person to act in a fairer manner toward you	• You are realistic about the degree of unfairness in the other person's behavior • You think that the other person has acted badly rather than as demonstrating lack of caring or showing indifference • You do not see yourself as alone, uncared for, or misunderstood • You are less likely to think of past "hurts" • You do not think that the other has to make the first move

Adversity	Belief	Emotion	Behavior	Subsequent Thinking
Threat to your relationship with your partner from another person	Irrational	Problematic jealousy	• You seek constant reassurance that you are loved • You monitor the actions and feelings of your partner • You search for evidence that your partner is involved with someone else • You attempt to restrict the movements or activities of your partner • You set tests that your partner has to pass • You retaliate for your partner's presumed infidelity • You sulk	• You tend to see threats to your relationship when none really exist • You think the loss of your relationship is imminent • You misconstrue your partner's ordinary conversations with relevant others as having romantic or sexual connotations • You construct visual images of your partner's infidelity • If your partner admits to finding another person attractive, you think that he or she finds that person more attractive than you and that he or she will leave you for this other person
Threat to your relationship with your partner from another person	Rational	Non-problematic jealousy	• You allow your partner to express love for you without seeking reassurance • You allow your partner freedom without monitoring his or her feelings, actions, and whereabouts • You allow your partner to show natural interest in members of the opposite sex without setting tests	• You tend not to see threats to your relationship when none exist • You do not misconstrue ordinary conversations between your partner and relevent others • You do not construct visual images of your partner's infidelity • You accept that your partner will find others attractive, but you do not see this as a threat

115

Adversity	Belief	Emotion	Behavior	Subsequent Thinking
Another person possesses and enjoys something desirable that you do not have	Irrational	Problematic envy	• You disparage to others the person who has the desired possession • You disparage to others the desired possession • If you had the chance, you would take away the desired possession from the other (either so that you will have it or that the other is deprived of it) • If you had the chance, you would spoil or destroy the desired possession so that the other person does not have it	• You tend to denigrate in your mind the value of the desired possession and/or the person who possesses it • You try to convince yourself that you are happy with your possessions (although you are not) • You think about how to acquire the desired possession regardless of its usefulness • You think about how to deprive the other person of the desired possession • You think about how to spoil or destroy the other's desired possession
Another person possesses and enjoys something desirable that you do not have	Rational	Non-problematic envy	• You strive to obtain the desired possession if it is truly what you want	• You honestly admit to yourself that you desire the possession • You do not try to convince yourself that you are happy with your possessions when you are not • You think about how to obtain the desired possession because you desire it for healthy reasons • You can allow the other person to have and enjoy the desired possession without denigrating that person or the possession

| Appendix 2 | # THE DISTINCTIVE FEATURES OF RATIONAL EMOTIVE BEHAVIOR THERAPY |

As the general field of cognitive-behavior therapy (CBT) has matured, it has spawned a number of different approaches within this tradition. Accompanying this trend has been an increasing interest in what is distinctive about different approaches to CBT. Now that we have put forward the case for a unified approach to REBT, let us outline the distinctive features of this approach, which is a précis of a book-length work on the subject (Dryden, 2009b).

THE DISTINCTIVE THEORETICAL FEATURES OF REBT

1. It espouses postmodern relativism, which is antithetical to rigid and extreme views and holds that there is no absolute way of determining reality.

2. It has a unique position on human nature (see Table 4).

3. It puts forward a distinctive Situational ABC model that highlights key inferential aspects of A and argues that C can be emotive,

TABLE 4 Description of the Nine Basic Assumptions Concerning
Human Nature and REBT's Position on These Continua

Freedom–Determinism

How much internal freedom do people have, and how far are they determined by external and internal (e.g., biological) factors?

REBT's position: Moderate emphasis toward the freedom end of the continuum.

Rationality–Irrationality

To what extent are people primarily rational, directing themselves through reason, and to what extent are they guided by irrational factors?

REBT's position: Mid-range between the two. People have the capacity to be both rational and irrational. They have to work harder to be rational than irrational.

Holism–Elementalism

To what extent are people best comprehended as a whole, and to what extent by being broken down into their constituent parts?

REBT's position: Moderate emphasis toward the holism end of the continuum.

Constitutionalism–Environmentalism

To what extent are people the result of constitutional factors, and to what extent are they products of environmental influences?

REBT's position: Strong emphasis toward the constitutionalism end of the continuum.

Changeability–Unchangeability

To what extent are people capable of fundamental change over time?

REBT's position: Moderate emphasis toward the changeability end of the continuum.

From L. A. Hjelle and D. J. Ziegler, *Personality theories: Basic assumptions, research and applications*, 1992, New York: McGraw-Hill. Adapted by permission.

Subjectivity–Objectivity

To what extent are people influenced by subjective factors and to what extent by external, objective factors?

REBT's position: Strong emphasis toward the subjectivity end of the continuum.

Proactivity–Reactivity

To what extent do people generate their behavior internally (proactivity), and to what extent do they respond to external stimuli (reactivity)?

REBT's position: Strong emphasis toward the proactivity end of the continuum.

Homeostasis–Heterostasis

To what extent are humans motivated primarily to reduce tensions and maintain an inner homeostasis, and to what extent are they motivated to actualize themselves?

REBT's position: Mid-range between the two.

Knowability–Unknowability

To what extent is human nature fully knowable?

REBT's position: Moderate emphasis toward the unknowability end of the continuum.

---

behavioral, and cognitive in nature. It also stresses that ABC's are best understood within a situational context.

4. It holds that rigid beliefs are at the core of psychological disturbance.

5. It holds that flexibility is at the core of psychological health.

6. It argues that extreme beliefs (awfulizing beliefs, discomfort-intolerance beliefs, and depreciation beliefs) are derived from rigid beliefs.

7. It argues that nonextreme beliefs (nonawfulizing beliefs, discomfort-tolerance beliefs, and acceptance beliefs) are derived from flexible beliefs.

8. It distinguishes between unhealthy (dysfunctional) negative emotions (UNEs) and healthy (functional) negative emotions (HNEs). For example, guilt (UNE) is distinguished from remorse (HNE).

9. It can explain why some clients' inferences are highly distorted (i.e., they are so when they are cognitive consequences of irrational beliefs).

10. It has a unique position on human worth and advocates unconditional self-acceptance (USA).

11. It distinguishes between ego and discomfort disturbance and health, but notes that they often interact.

12. It has a decided focus on meta-emotional disturbance (e.g., shame for feeling unhealthy anger).

13. It argues that the biological basis of human irrationality is often stronger that its social learning basis.

14. It favors what might be called *choice-based constructivism* and argues that humans frequently have to go against the grain when striving for therapeutic change. Thus humans can choose to construct a set of rational beliefs and go against the grain by acting in ways that strengthen such beliefs.

15. It has a clear position on what constitutes good mental health, with flexibility and nonextremeness at its heart.

THE DISTINCTIVE PRACTICAL FEATURES OF REBT

1. It argues that the therapeutic relationship in REBT is important but not curative and draws fully on working alliance theory (Bordin, 1979) as a way of understanding the importance of bonds, views, goals, and tasks in therapy.

2. It takes a flexible approach to case formulation, using this to guide interventions, particularly in complex cases. However, it argues that one can do good therapy without making such a formulation and holds that frequently this formulation can be developed during therapy, rather than fully at its outset.

3. It has a decided psychoeducational emphasis and argues that its theory of disturbance and of change can actively be taught to and implemented by clients.

4. It has a preferred order of treatment and argues that client problems should ideally be dealt with in the following order: (1) disturbance, (2) dissatisfaction, and (3) development.

5. It advocates an early focus on clients' irrational beliefs (iB's).

6. It does not just suggest disputing clients' iB's; it also encourages clients to develop and strengthen rational beliefs (rB's).

7. In keeping with other CBT approaches, it uses empirical and pragmatic arguments in disputing beliefs, but uniquely it also uses logical arguments.

8. It suggests using a variety of therapeutic styles.

9. It discourages the use of gradualism (i.e., proceeding very slowly), as this often reinforces clients' discomfort-tolerance beliefs.

10. It has a realistic view of change and encourages clients to accept that change is hard work; consequently, it urges therapists to be forceful and energetic as long as doing so does not threaten the therapeutic alliance.

11. It stresses, whenever possible, the importance of teaching clients general rational philosophies and encourages them to make a "profound philosophic change" (changing general iB's to general rB's) if they are capable of doing so.

12. It recognizes that clients may not be able or willing to change their iB's, and in such cases it recommends making compromises with the ideal of belief change.

13. It suggests that therapists focus on their clients' misconceptions, doubts, reservations, and objections to REBT.

14. It recommends the principle of therapeutic efficiency: bringing about change in the briefest time possible.

15. It is a form of theoretically consistent eclecticism, advocating the broad use of techniques from varied sources but in the interest of achieving goals in keeping with REBT theory.

REFERENCES AND RECOMMENDED READING

Bard, J. A. (1980). *Rational-emotive therapy in practice*. Champaign, IL: Research Press.

Bordin, E. S. (1979). The generalizability of the psychoanalytic concept of the working alliance. *Psychotherapy: Theory, Research and Practice, 16*, 252–260.

Crawford, T., & Ellis, A. (1989). A dictionary of rational-emotive feelings and behaviors. *Journal of Rational-Emotive and Cognitive-Behavior Therapy, 7*, 3–27.

Dryden, W. (1986). Language and meaning in RET. *Journal of Rational-Emotive Therapy, 4*, 131–142.

Dryden, W. (1990). Self-disclosure in rational-emotive therapy. In G. Stricker & M. N. Fisher (Eds.), *Self-disclosure in the therapeutic relationship*. New York, NY: Plenum.

Dryden, W. (2000). The "friend dispute." In M. E. Bernard & J. L. Wolfe (Eds.), *The REBT resource book for practitioners* (2nd ed.). New York, NY: Albert Ellis Institute.

Dryden, W. (2006). *Counselling in a nutshell*. London, England: Sage.

Dryden, W. (2009a). *Understanding emotional problems: The REBT perspective*. Hove, East Sussex, England: Routledge.

Dryden, W. (2009b). *Rational emotive behaviour therapy: Distinctive features.* London, England: Routledge.

Dryden, W., & Neenan, M. (2004). *Counselling individuals: A rational emotive behavioural handbook.* London, England: Whurr.

Ellis, A. (1962). *Reason and emotion in psychotherapy.* Secaucus, NJ: Citadel.

Ellis, A. (1976). The biological basis of human irrationality. *Journal of Individual Psychology, 32,* 145–168.

Ellis, A. (1984a). The essence of RET—1984. *Journal of Rational-Emotive Therapy, 2,* 19–25.

Ellis, A. (1984b). *How to maintain and enhance your rational-emotive therapy gains.* New York, NY: Albert Ellis Institute.

Ellis, A. (1985). Expanding the ABC's of rational-emotive therapy. In M. J. Mahoney & A. Freeman (Eds.), *Cognition and psychotherapy* (pp. 313–323). New York, NY: Plenum.

Ellis, A. (1988). *How to stubbornly refuse to make yourself miserable about any-thing—Yes, anything!* Secaucus, NJ: Lyle Stuart.

Ellis, A. (1994). *Reason and emotion in psychotherapy* (Rev. ed.). Secaucus, NJ: Carol.

Ellis, A. (1999). *How to make yourself happy and remarkably less disturbable.* San Luis Obispo, CA: Impact.

Ellis, A. (2000). *Feeling better, getting better, staying better.* San Luis Obispo, CA: Impact.

Ellis, A. (2002). *Overcoming resistance: A rational emotive behavior therapy inte-grated approach* (2nd ed.). New York, NY: Springer.

Ellis, A., & Dryden, W. (1997). *The practice of rational emotive behavior therapy* (2nd ed.). New York, NY: Springer.

Gendlin, E. T. (1978). *Focusing.* New York, NY: Everest.

Hjelle, L. A., & Ziegler, D. J. (1992). *Personality theories: Basic assumptions, research and applications.* New York, NY: McGraw-Hill.

Maultsby, M. C., Jr., & Ellis, A. (1974). *Techniques for using rational-emotive imagery.* New York, NY: Albert Ellis Institute.

Neenan, M. (2009). *Developing resilience: A cognitive behavioural approach.* Hove, East Sussex, England: Routledge.

Passons, W. R. (1975). *Gestalt approaches in counseling.* New York, NY: Holt, Rinehart & Winston.

Trexler, L. D. (1976). Frustration is a fact, not a feeling. *Rational Living, 11*(2), 19–22.

Walen, S. R., DiGiuseppe, R., & Dryden, W. (1992). *A practitioner's guide to rational-emotive therapy* (2nd ed.). New York, NY: Oxford University Press.

ABOUT THE AUTHORS

Windy Dryden is professor of psychotherapeutic studies at Goldsmiths, University of London, and is a Fellow of the British Psychological Society and of the British Association for Counselling and Psychotherapy. He has authored or edited more than 170 books, including *Counselling in a Nutshell* (Sage, 2006) and *Rational Emotive Behaviour Therapy: Distinctive Features* (Routledge, 2009b). In addition, he edits 18 book series in the area of counseling and psychotherapy, including the *Distinctive Features in CBT* series (Routledge) and the *Counselling in a Nutshell* series (Sage). His major interests are in rational emotive behavior therapy, eclecticism and integration in psychotherapy, and writing short, accessible self-help books for the general public.

After earning a BS degree from Villanova University, **Raymond DiGiuseppe** received his PhD from Hofstra University in 1975. He completed a postdoctoral fellowship at the Albert Ellis Institute in 1977. Ray joined the faculty of St. John's University in 1987, where he developed a doctoral program in school psychology and received the university's Faculty Achievement Medal. He currently is professor and chair of psychology at St. John's. Since 1980, Ray has served as director of professional education at the Albert Ellis Institute. He has trained hundreds of therapists from around the world in cognitive-behavior therapy (CBT). He received the Jack Krasner Early Career Contribution Award from the American Psychological Association's (APA) Division of Psychotherapy and was elected a Fellow of the APA's divisions of psychotherapy and of clinical, school, and family psychology. Ray has had a history of service since joining the Association for Behavioral and Cognitive Therapies (ABCT). He helped develop the Diplomat in Behavioral Psychology (1986–1987) and served on the Diplomat Board. He was associate program chair of ABCT's 1995 convention, and program chair in 1996. He served on the founding editorial board of ABCT's journal *Cognitive and Behavioral Practice*. As convention coordinator (1997–2000) and associate convener of the World Congress (2001), Ray developed and promoted popular convention formats such as the Master Clinician series and the World Rounds demonstrations. He was elected representative-at-large in 2001 and served as president of the organization in 2006–2007. Ray has been involved in the APA's Division of Psychotherapy, in which he has served on the division's publication board and on the editorial board of *Psychotherapy: Theory, Research, Practice, Supervision*. Ray has contributed to the scientific and clinical literature with six books, more than a hundred chapters and articles, and more than a hundred conference presentations. He has published the Anger Disorders Scale with Raymond Chip Tafrate, and they are working on the Anger Disorder Scale for Youth. Ray's current scholarship focuses on clinical aspects of anger, on which he lectures widely.

Michael Neenan is associate director of the Center for Stress Management in London, England, an accredited cognitive behavior therapist, and author of *Developing Resilience: A Cognitive Behavioural Approach* (Routledge, 2009). He has coauthored eight books on REBT, as well as more than 25 articles and chapters. He coedits the *Rational Emotive Behaviour Therapist*, the journal of the Association for Rational Emotive Behaviour Therapy (United Kingdom).